THE INVENTOR'S NOTEBOOK

■

by Fred Grissom & David Pressman

Edited by Stephen Elias

IMPORTANT UPDATE INFORMATION

Legislation pending in Congress as of July 1995 would affect the information we provide in this publication about the length of the utility patent term. Also, the U.S. Patent and Trademark Office anticipates the introduction and passage of a new law that will require the publication of patent applications 18 months after they are filed. This would affect the information we provide about maintaining an invention as a trade secret when prosecuting the patent.

To stay informed about these and other important developments in the patent field, read the *Nolo News* update column or visit our update service at one of the following on-line sites:

- WWW (Internet): http://gnn.com/gnn/bus/nolo/
- America Online: (key word Nolo)
- eWorld: (key word Nolo)

NOLO PRESS BERKELEY

YOUR RESPONSIBILITY WHEN USING A SELF-HELP LAW BOOK

We've done our best to give you useful and accurate information in this book. But laws and procedures change frequently and are subject to differing interpretations. If you want legal advice backed by a guarantee, see a lawyer. If you use this book, it's your responsibility to make sure that the facts and general advice contained in it are applicable to your situation.

KEEPING UP-TO-DATE

To keep its books up-to-date, Nolo Press issues new printings and new editions periodically. New printings reflect minor legal changes and technical corrections. New editions contain major legal changes, major text additions or major reorganizations. To find out if a later printing or edition of any Nolo book is available, call Nolo Press at 510-549-1976 or check the catalog in the *Nolo News,* our quarterly newspaper.

To stay current, follow the "Update" service in the *Nolo News.* You can get a free two-year subscription by sending us the registration card in the back of the book. In another effort to help you use Nolo's latest materials, we offer a 25% discount off the purchase of any new Nolo book if you turn in any earlier printing or edition. (See the "Recycle Offer" in the back of the book.)

This book was last revised in: **July 1995.**

FIRST EDITION	September 1987
FIFTH PRINTING	July 1995
ILLUSTRATIONS	Linda Allison
PRODUCTION	Stephanie Harolde
BOOK DESIGN & LAYOUT	Jackie Mancuso Toni Ihara Keija Kimura
PRINTING	Delta Lithograph

Printed in the U.S.A. Printed on paper with recycled content
Library of Congress Catalog Card Number: 87-62287. ISBN 87337-049-X

DEDICATION

To our wives—Shelley, for her faith and sense of humor, and Roberta, for her perserverance and style.

ABOUT NOLO PRESS

The leading publisher of self-help law books and software since 1971

Nolo Press exists because two former Legal Aid lawyers, fed up with the public's lack of affordable legal information and advice, began writing understandable, easy-to-use, self-help law books more than 20 years ago. Now, Nolo publishes books, form kits, software and audio- and videotapes. But the purpose has never changed: to take the mystery out of law and make it available to everyone.

About 60 of us work in a converted clock factory in Berkeley, California. We regularly tackle new self-help law products and, because laws change constantly, work to keep our backlist (80 titles) up-to-date. We encourage our customers to suggest ideas for improvement, which we can incorporate into new editions.

Lawyers sometimes compare self-help law to do-it-yourself brain surgery. Nonsense—it's much more akin to choosing an over-the-counter remedy for a routine illness. Whether they want to relieve a headache, prepare their income tax returns, build a room on a house or handle their own bankruptcy case, people can do much of the work themselves if they have good reliable information.

Twenty years' experience has only strengthened our belief that law, like any other body of information, can be broken down and organized into small, easily-digested bits. Once that's done, it's relatively easy to find answers to legal questions, whether they concern a divorce, trademark or dog bite dispute.

Nolo's mission is far from a radical idea. Every American's right to know the law—without paying a lawyer—is a cornerstone of our democracy. Making the process easier is what we are here for.

ACKNOWLEDGEMENTS

The authors wish to express their thanks and appreciation to Jake Warner and Steve Elias of Nolo Press for their invaluable advice and sustaining enthusiasm, the rest of the crew at Nolo—especially Mary Randolph, Jackie Clark, David Cole, Toni Ihara and Carol Pladsen—for their respective creative contributions to the design and marketing of this notebook. We also thank Paul Guyton and David Joyner for stoking the creative fires with their critical insights, and Andromache Warner for her valuable advice on doing market research.

ABOUT THE AUTHORS

FRED GRISSOM

Fred Grissom, a graduate of the University of Texas, has developed and implemented high technology training programs around the world, and worked as a new product design engineer for computer simulation equipment. Fred is a business development consultant, an active member of the Houston Inventor's Association and a member of the Texas Technology Transfer Association. He is currently employed by Lockheed Engineering and Science Company as a Management Systems Specialist in support of NASA's Technology Utilization Program at the Johnson Space Center.

DAVID PRESSMAN

David Pressman is a member of the Pennsylvania, California, and Patent And Trademark Office bars. He has had over 25 years' experience in the patent profession, as a patent examiner for the U.S. Patent Office, a patent attorney for Philco-Ford Corp., Elco Corp., and Varian Associates, as a columnist for EDN Magazine, and as an instructor at San Francisco State University. When not writing, he practices as a patent lawyer in San Francisco. Originally from Philadelphia, he has a BS in EE from Penn State University and a JD from George Washington University. A member of Mensa, he is also active in the general semantics and vegetarian movements.

TABLE OF CONTENTS

What The Inventor's Notebook Does and How to Use It

There are four main activities that all successful inventors must normally undertake:

• conceiving, building and testing the invention;

• legally protecting the invention;

• marketing the invention; and

• financing the first three tasks.

The Inventor's Notebook is designed to help you organize the records you need to successfully complete of each of these activities. Specifically, *The Inventor's Notebook* will show you how to document the details of your invention in order to:

• maintain good records of your inventing process. By doing this you will always know exactly where you are in the invention process and what remains to be done. This will help you avoid dead-ends and the repetition of mistakes;

• create a legal record that you are the first and true inventor. If your invention is ever challenged, your completed notebook will be the foundation of the legal protection for your idea;

• convince others of the worth of your invention;

• proceed realistically in terms of your invention's commercial potential; and

• organize all the information pertaining to your invention in one location.

A. BRIEF DESCRIPTION OF THE INVENTOR'S NOTEBOOK

The Inventor's Notebook is designed for a single invention. You should use a separate notebook for each invention. *The Inventor's Notebook* consists of:

• Part A—The Work Diary

• Part B—Legal Protection

• Part C—Marketing

• Part D—Financing

A part with blank pages (Part E) which allow you to continue entries begun in one of the four main workbook parts if you run out of room;

A bibliography (Part F); and

Tear-out forms (Part G) which help you determine the commercial feasibility of your invention and maintain its confidentiality prior to its receiving a patent.

The beginning of each of these workbook parts contains a brief overview of what's in it. We provide instructions for completing the forms in the part at the beginning of each section. We also provide one or two specific references for additional background reading.

In some instances we offer you several copies of each form. This is because, as you know, the inventive process is interactive and commonly gives rise to more than one version of the invention. These versions are usually harmonized before you file your patent application, but until this occurs it is essential that you record the details of each version.

B. SCOPE OF THE INVENTOR'S NOTEBOOK

The purpose of *The Inventor's Notebook* is to provide you with an organized means for documenting your inventive efforts. We do not explain here the details of patent law or the intricacies of how to create and run a business based on your invention.[1] Nolo Press already publishes *Patent It Yourself,* an excellent source of detailed information on obtaining and using a patent.[2] In fact, throughout *The Inventor's Notebook* we provide cross references to the relevant portions of *Patent It Yourself* and feature some of its "Inventor's Commandments" where appropriate.[3] We also suggest that you consult *How to Write a Business Plan* by Michael McKeever (Nolo Press).

---

[1] Before devoting your time, energy and economic resources to an invention, it is appropriate to figure out the relationship between what you might put into the invention and what you expect to get out of it. In this sense, launching an invention is the same as starting a business; in both situations you should carefully calculate your profit potential before you get in too deeply. It is this activity that we refer to when we later speak of creating a business plan for your invention.

[2] Editor's Note: For a full understanding of the legal principles associated with the information you will be entering in *The Inventor's Notebook,* we recommend that you obtain a copy of this comprehensive and clearly written resource. It is widely available in libraries and bookstores and can be obtained by sending in the coupon order located in the middle of the book.

[3] In *Patent It Yourself,* author David Pressman has formulated sixteen statements or instructions (termed Inventor's Commandments) that focus the reader's attention on the crucial steps necessary to the successful development of his or her invention.

C. HOW THE INVENTOR'S NOTEBOOK IS ORGANIZED

The Inventor's Notebook is designed to focus your attention on all major activities associated with successful inventing, and on the documentation which is appropriate and necessary to each. As our organizing tool we use the Inventor's Decision Chart from *Patent It Yourself.*

As you can see, the chart presents a concise overview of the basic steps of the inventive process.

In the real world, of course, there can be a great many ways in which an invention goes from idea to marketplace. However, the paths outlined in the Inventor's Decision Chart serve as logical guidelines to the way in which a large percentage of inventing efforts will tend to develop, primarily because the fundamental questions addressed by the chart—legal protection, financial feasibility, marketing potential, and perfecting the final design of the product—must be addressed in most instances.

At the end of this introduction, we offer a brief description of the different paths represented in the Inventor's Decision Chart. A more extensive discussion can be found in *Patent It Yourself.*

D. HOW TO USE THE INVENTOR'S NOTEBOOK

The four workbook parts of *The Inventor's Notebook* (Parts A-D) are keyed to the boxes on the Inventor's Decision Chart. This is because almost every box on the chart calls for a specific type of documentation. Sometimes the documentation you need to supply will consist of a running description of the details of the invention (what nuts go on what bolts). Other times the documentation must be entered on a chart or checklist we provide.

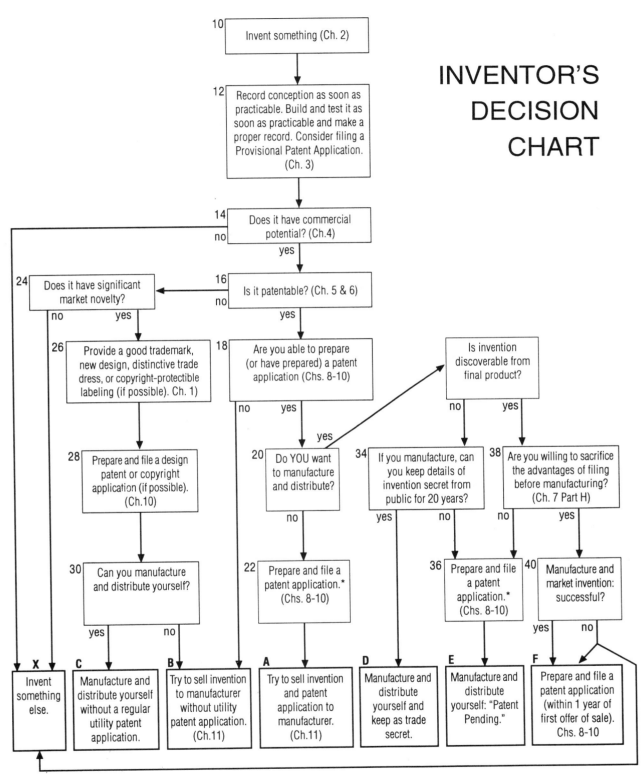

INVENTOR'S DECISION CHART

10 Invent something (Ch. 2)

12 Record conception as soon as practicable. Build and test it as soon as practicable and make a proper record. Consider filing a Provisional Patent Application. (Ch. 3)

14 Does it have commercial potential? (Ch.4) — no

16 Is it patentable? (Ch. 5 & 6) — no / yes

24 Does it have significant market novelty? — no / yes

26 Provide a good trademark, new design, distinctive trade dress, or copyright-protectible labeling (if possible). Ch. 1

28 Prepare and file a design patent or copyright application (if possible). (Ch.10)

30 Can you manufacture and distribute yourself? — yes / no

18 Are you able to prepare (or have prepared) a patent application (Chs. 8-10) — no / yes

20 Do YOU want to manufacture and distribute? — no

22 Prepare and file a patent application.* (Chs. 8-10)

Is invention discoverable from final product? — no / yes

34 If you manufacture, can you keep details of invention secret from public for 20 years? — yes / no

38 Are you willing to sacrifice the advantages of filing before manufacturing? (Ch. 7 Part H) — no / yes

36 Prepare and file a patent application.* (Chs. 8-10)

40 Manufacture and market invention: successful? — yes / no

X Invent something else.

C Manufacture and distribute yourself without a regular utility patent application.

B Try to sell invention to manufacturer without utility patent application. (Ch.11)

A Try to sell invention and patent application to manufacturer. (Ch.11)

D Manufacture and distribute yourself and keep as trade secret.

E Manufacture and distribute yourself: "Patent Pending."

F Prepare and file a patent application (within 1 year of first offer of sale). Chs. 8-10

*If you filed a Provisional Patent Application, you *must* file a regular patent application and any desired foreign convention applications within one year—see Ch.3. (File non-convention applications before invention is made public or any patent issues on it.)

Below is a Table of Cross-References, which ties each box on the chart to the relevant part and section or sections of the notebook.

Table of Cross References

INVENTOR'S DECISION CHART	INVENTOR'S NOTEBOOK SECTIONS	PATENT IT YOURSELF CHAPTERS
#10	A1, A3, B6	1, 2
#12	A1, A2, A3, B6, C1, D1	1, 3
#14	C1, C2, C3, A3, D1	4
#16	B1, B2	5
#18	B3, B6,B7, D1	1,8
#20	C5, D1, D3, C4	11
#22	B1, B2, B3, B7	6, 8, 9, 10, 12, 13, 14, 15
#24	C1, B1, C2, C3	4
#26	A4, A5, B5	1
#28	A5, B4	10
#30	C5, D1, D3, C4	11
#32	B6, B7	1
#34	B6,B7	1
#36	B3, B7	6, 8, 9, 10, 12, 13, 14, 15
#38	D1, C4, B7	7
#40	—	7
A	C5, D2, B7	11, 15, 16
B	C5, D2, B1,B7	1, 11
C	—	1, 11
D	B6	1, 11
E	B6	1, 11, 15
F	B3	6, 8, 9, 10, 12, 13, 14, 15
X	Begin a new Inventor's Notebook	2

To see how this cross reference table works, assume you have conceived an invention (Box 10) and now are at Box 12 of the inventive process (record conception as soon as practicable, build and test it as soon as practicable and make a proper record, or consider filing a Provisional Patent Application). The Table of Cross References tells you that Sections A1 (Documentation of Conception), A2 (Documentation of Building and Testing or filing a Provisional Patent Application), A3 (Trademark Conception), B6 (Record of Contacts), C1 (Commercial Evaluation) and D1 (Estimation of Necessary Funding) of the notebook need your attention.

Now let's take a brief look at what each of these notebook sections listed in the chart for this example calls for.

HOW TO RECORD YOUR INVENTION—A1

Section A1 provides specific guidelines as to how to record your conception.

RECORD THE BUILDING AND TESTING OF YOUR INVENTION—A2

This section explains the importance of recording your efforts to build and test your invention and contains eight grid-lined pages (with inventor and witness signature lines at the bottom of each page) for this purpose. The better this documentation, the easier it will be for you to apply for a patent and the better your legal position will be if:

- you ever get into an inventorship dispute (one person claims that another person stole the invention from the first person);

- an interference is declared (a contest initiated in the Patent and Trademark Office when two patent applications from different inventors claim the same invention); or

- you need to swear behind a cited reference (i.e., show that you conceived or built and tested the invention before the date of a reference that would otherwise be "prior art" to your invention).[4]

FILE A PROVISIONAL PATENT APPLICATION— A2 (OPTIONAL)

As of June 8, 1995, an inventor can file a Provisional Patent Application (PPA) as an alternative to building and testing the invention. The PPA will be examined only if the inventor files a regular patent application that claims the same invention disclosed in the PPA is filed within one year. If the PPA disclosure is deemed sufficient by the patent examiner, the regular application may claim the PPA's filing date.

---

[4]When determining whether your invention is sufficiently innovative under the Patent Act (i.e., that it's novel and non-obvious), the Patent and Trademark Office (PTO) and your adversaries in any court case will examine all known references that bear on your claims. It is very important to show that your earliest effective date of invention (patent application filing date, building and testing date, or date when you first began to diligently work towards building and testing) occurred prior to all such references; otherwise, your claims can be rejected on them.

OTHER POSSIBLE APPLICATIONS—A3

This section asks you to focus on possible applications of your work which differ from those you have imagined.

RECORD OF CONTACTS—B6

This section permits you to keep track of all the people who know of your invention and who have signed confidentiality agreements. This information will be essential if a dispute arises later over inventorship or you wish to take action against others under the trade secret laws for violation of a confidentiality agreement.[5]

EVALUATION OF POSITIVE AND NEGATIVE FACTORS OF INVENTION—C1

This section guides you in evaluating the positive and negative factors of your invention so that you can make refinements while building and testing it.

DETERMINATION OF FUNDS NEEDED—D1

Finally this section lets you document any special financial needs for your building and testing phase.

---

[5]Many inventors maintain their invention as a trade secret until such time as a patent issues or the invention is manufactured and placed on the market. This allows the inventor to take action against anyone who discloses the details of the invention to others in violation of a confidentiality agreement.

To sum up this example, Box 12 of the Table of Cross References directs you to the parts of the notebook you should use for recording your conception and documenting the building and testing of your invention. As you proceed through the chart, other boxes will similarly direct you to other appropriate parts of the notebook. Careful documentation of your invention process will save time in the long run. Your organized approach will make it easy to retrieve essential information when you need it, and you will be able to prove your inventorship if called on to do so.

Direct Access Note: You can directly access *The Inventor's Notebook* without going through the Inventor's Decision Chart if you already understand what documentation is needed. Simply turn to the relevant portion of the notebook and enter the appropriate information. For guidance on the type of documentation needed to protect your invention, read the relevant portions of *Patent It Yourself* (or other resources recommended by us) which are referenced in a special box at the beginning of each section in the work diary portion of the notebook.

Warning: You are responsible for understanding the legal requirements for documentation and what steps have to be taken to obtain a patent and protect your invention from theft or unauthorized use. While we preface each section with a very brief overview of what should be entered there, and why it should be entered, this is not a substitute for reading the meticulous discussion of these issues provided by *Patent It Yourself*.

E. EXPLANATION OF INVENTOR'S DECISION CHART

As we mentioned, different inventions take different paths through the Inventor's Decision Chart. Here we outline the various paths. If you are not using the Inventor's Decision Chart as an organizational guide to this notebook, you may skip this discussion.

1. DROP IT IF YOU DON'T SEE COMMERCIAL POTENTIAL (CHART ROUTE 10-12-14-X)

If you've invented something (Box 10 of the chart) and recorded it properly (Box 12), you should then proceed to build and test your invention as soon as practicable and/or optionally file a Provisional Patent Application and then file a regular patent application within one year that claims the PPA filing date. (Box 12). If you choose to build and test the invention and this presents appreciable difficulty, you should wait until after you evaluate your invention's commercial potential (Box 14) or patentability (Box 16). But always keep the building and testing as a goal; it will help you to evaluate commercial potential and may be vital in the event an "interference"[6] occurs unless you file a valid PPA (see Part A2 for a discussion on what makes a PPA valid). What's more, you'll find a working model extremely valuable when you show the invention to a manufacturer.

Your next step, stated in Box 14, is to investigate your invention's commercial potential. Assuming you decide that your invention has no commercial potential and you answer the questions no, follow an arrow to Box X, which says "Invent something else." In this instance, this sort of structured analysis may seem simplistic. It's not. In our direct experience we have seen hundreds of inventors waste thousands of hours because they would not

---

[6]An interference is a proceeding in the PTO which is instituted when two or more applications by separate inventors claim the same invention. It usually occurs when a patent examiner in the PTO discovers two pending applications which claim the same invention. It can also occur when the PTO publishes a newly granted patent in the *Official Gazette* and another inventor claims to have invented it first. Since interferences are long and expensive proceedings, the more convincing a party's documentation is, the better the chance to win and shorten an interference.

confront the issue of "commercial potential" or lack thereof at an early stage of the invention process.

2. TRY TO SELL INVENTION TO MANUFACTURER WITHOUT "REGULAR" PATENT APPLICATION (CHART ROUTE 12-14-16-18-B

This route is especially useful if you've filed a PPA on the invention (Box 12) but can also be used if you've built and tested the invention and properly recorded your building and testing activities. After filing a PPA and/or building and testing and recording your efforts (Box 12), see if the invention has commercial potential (Box 14) and if it's patentable (Box 16). If so, whether or not you're able to prepare—or have prepared—a regular patent application, try to sell your invention to a manufacturer (Box B) in the hope that the manufacturer will have the application prepared for you, either on the basis of your PPA or without the PPA. If you take this route, you should be sure either that your PPA is properly prepared or that you've properly documented conception, building and testing. We recommend this route only if you can't prepare or can't afford to have prepared a regular patent application because:

• if you've only built and tested the invention without properly recording your activities, you run a risk of an unscrupulous manufacturer stealing your invention by filing a patent application on your invention before you do so, and

• if you've filed a PPA, you'll have all of the disadvantages of the PPA (see Part A2 for more discussion of the advantages and disadvantages of filing a PPA).

3. FILE A PATENT APPLICATION AND SELL OR LICENSE IT TO A MANUFACTURER (CHART ROUTE 14-16-18-20-22-A)

Filing a patent application and selling rights to the invention to someone else is the usual way most inventors profit from their work. This is because inventors seldom have the capability (and often don't have the desire) to establish their own manufacturing and distribution facilities. If you are in this situation, the chart works like this:

• Box 14—your invention has good commercial potential

• Box 16—your decision on patentability is favorable

• Box 18—you're able to prepare a regular patent application (or have one prepared for you), and

• Box 20—you don't wish to manufacture and distribute your product or process yourself

• Box 22—you prepare a regular patent application

• Box A—you try to sell your invention (and accompanying patent application) to a manufacturer.

4. SELL OR LICENSE YOUR INVENTION TO A MANUFACTURER WITHOUT FILING A PATENT APPLICATION (CHART ROUTE 16-24-26-28-30-B)

If your invention isn't patentable (i.e., the decision in Box 16 is negative), don't give up. There's still hope that you can profit from your work. If your invention nevertheless possesses "significant market novelty" (Box 24), it may in fact be quite profitable if introduced to the market. Put differently, if your patentability search produces close prior art[7] (but not a dead ringer), this may indicate that no one has tried to market your specific idea before. For example, the prior art which precludes you from getting a patent may have only been used to make computer screens, while your invention is designed for lamp shades.

---

[7]Prior art is the sum of all developments prior to your conception which are used to determine whether your efforts were really inventive or not different enough to be considered "unobvious." Examples of prior art (relevant to your invention) are (1) prior patents showing your invention or any part or feature of it, (2) prior and related technological developments which are known to the public, (3) previous descriptions of your invention (or any part or feature of it) in periodicals or textbooks, and (4) previous indications of any kind that others considered some or all of your invention's elements.

Assuming that your invention does have significant market novelty but does not qualify for protection under a utility patent,[8] you may consider protecting it under trademark law (Box 26), a design patent (Box 28), or through distinctive "trade dress," such as a special, uniform color (as *Kodak* does with its yellow film packages), or a symbol (such as the McDonalds golden arch).

5. **MAKE AND SELL YOUR INVENTION YOURSELF WITHOUT A UTILITY PATENT APPLICATION (CHART ROUTE 30-C)**

Here we assume again that you have an unpatentable invention which at the same time is unique and serves a useful purpose (there isn't anything on the market just like it and people will buy it). If you can make and distribute it yourself (Box 30), it may be better to do so (Box C) than to try to sell it to a manufacturer outright. Even if you have a good trademark, a design patent application, distinctive trade dress, and/or a unique label, you cannot offer a manufacturer a truly privileged market position on your invention unless it's covered by a utility patent application that looks like it will lead to a patent being granted. This means it will probably be hard to sell your invention to a third party, and if you do, the amount you receive for it will be modest. However, if you decide to manufacture the invention yourself, and you reach the market first, you'll have a significant marketing advantage despite the lack of a utility patent.

6. **MANUFACTURE AND DISTRIBUTE YOUR INVENTION YOURSELF, KEEPING IT AS A TRADE SECRET (CHART ROUTE 20-32-34-D)**

Even though your invention may be commercially valuable and patentable, it isn't always in your best interest to patent it. Instead you may profit more by keeping the invention secret and using it in your business to obtain a competitive advantage. For instance, suppose you invent a formula that truly makes hair grow. Instead of seeking a patent, which would require public

---

[8]Most patents are utility patents, granted on the functional aspects of inventions.

disclosure of your formula and invite others to figure out why your formula works and perhaps invent alternatives, you might be better off keeping your formula locked in your safe and only disclose it to a few trusted associates who would be sworn to secrecy. For more on trade secret protection for inventions, see Chapter 1 of *Patent It Yourself.*

7. FILE PATENT APPLICATION AND MANUFACTURE AND DISTRIBUTE YOUR INVENTION YOURSELF (TRADE-SECRETABLE INVENTION) (CHART ROUTE 20-32-34-36-E)

Suppose the essence of your invention is not easily discoverable from your final product (Box 32) so that you could keep it secret for a while, but probably not for the life of a patent (Box 34). Or, suppose, after evaluating the advantages and disadvantages of maintaining your invention as a trade secret (Section 5 above), you decide against the trade secret protection route, preferring instead to patent your invention. Either way, you should prepare and file a patent application (Box 36) and then manufacture and distribute the invention yourself with the notice "patent pending" affixed to the invention (Box E).

8. FILE PATENT APPLICATION AND MANUFACTURE AND DISTRIBUTE INVENTION YOURSELF (NON-TRADE SECRETABLE INVENTION) (CHART ROUTE 20-32-38-36-E)

This is the route followed by most inventors who wish to manufacture their own invention. Assume that the essence of your invention, like most, is discoverable from the final product (Box 32). In this case you won't be able to protect it as a trade secret. Also assume (Box 38) that you don't want to sacrifice the advantages of filing before manufacturing (see next part). You should prepare and file a patent application (Box 36) and then manufacture and distribute the invention yourself with a patent-pending notice (Box E).

9. TEST MARKET BEFORE FILING
(CHART ROUTE 20-32-38-40-F)

Although you might like to manufacture and test market your invention before filing a patent application on it, we generally don't recommend this for patentable inventions. This is because, under the "one-year rule," you have less than one year to do the test marketing before your patent application must be filed.[9] Since one year is a relatively short time, you may get discouraged unjustifiably if you try to market your invention and you aren't successful. Also, you'll lose your foreign rights since most foreign countries or jurisdictions, including the European Patent Office, have an "absolute novelty" requirement (which means no patent will be issued if the invention was made public anywhere before its first filing date). Lastly, there is a possibility of theft since anyone who sees it can (assuming it's not trade secretable) copy it and file a (fraudulent) patent application on it. There are also significant other disadvantages to test marketing an invention.

Nevertheless, you may still choose to manufacture and market your invention (Box 40) before filing your patent application. If you discover, within about nine months of the date you first introduce your product, that it is a successful invention and likely to have good commercial success, begin immediately to prepare your patent application (Box F), so that you'll be able to get it on file within one year from the date you first offered your invention for sale or used it to make a commercial product.

If your manufacturing and market tests (Box 40) are not successful, you should consider dropping the invention and inventing something else (Box X), even though you still have the right to get a patent on your invention. On the other hand, as we stated above, a 9-month testing period may not have been adequate. In other words, be realistic but don't get discouraged unnecessarily from filing a patent application.

---

[9]This very important rule is based upon a statute which states that, with certain exceptions, you must file your patent application within one year after the invention was exposed to the public.

PART A

The Work Diary

Part A: The Work Diary

WHAT'S IN IT

This part of *The Inventor's Notebook* contains the following sections:

• Record Your Conception (Section A1);

• Record the Building and Testing of Your Invention (Section A2);

• Other Possible Applications of Your Invention (Section A3);.

• Record Your Trademark Conception (Section A4); and

• Record Your Distinctive Design Conception (Section A5).

A well-maintained work diary will be of crucial importance should your inventorship or your eligibility for a patent ever be called into question by the Patent and Trademark Office, other inventors, or companies which you have sued for infringement.

HOW TO MAKE ENTRIES

When using this work diary, it is important to remember that the more secure your notebook appears to be from the possibility of after-the-fact modifications by you, the better evidence it is. The first step in achieving this credibility is to use a bound notebook like this one. Your textual entries, sketches and diagrams should be clearly written in ink to preclude erasure and the making of later entries. No large blank spaces should be left on a page. If you do need to leave space between separate entries, or at the bottom of a page, draw a large cross over the blank space to preclude the possibility of any subsequent entries. If you make a mistake in an entry, don't attempt to erase it; merely line it out neatly and make a dated note of why it was incorrect. Your entries should be worded carefully and accurately to be complete and clear in themselves so that a disinterested person could verify that you had the ideas or did the work stated on the dates in question.

Where we indicate, your entries in the work diary should be signed, dated and witnessed. This should be done frequently. You should date each entry the same day you (and your co-inventors if any) make the entries and sign your name(s). If it is impossible to have a witness sign the same day you do, add a brief candid comment to this effect when the witness does sign. Similarly, if you made and/or built the invention some time ago, but haven't made any records until now, again state the full and truthful facts and date the entry as of the date you write and sign it. Remember, though, that entries that are made contemporaneously with your work or ideas will carry much more weight than after-the-fact entries, should you ever have to prove prior inventorship.

If possible, items that by their nature can't be entered directly in the notebook by hand should be made on separate sheets. These, too, should be signed, dated and witnessed and then pasted or affixed in the notebook in proper chronological order. The inserted sheet should be referred to by entries made directly in the notebook, thus tying them in to the other material. Photos or other entries which cannot be signed or written should be pasted in the notebook and referenced by legends (descriptive words, such as "photo taken of machine in operation") made directly in the notebook, preferably with lead lines which extend from the notebook page over onto the photo, so as to preclude a charge of substituting subsequently made photos (see Fig. 3-B). The page the photo is pasted on should be signed dated, and witnessed in the usual manner.

If an item covers an entire page, it can be referred to on an adjacent page. It's important to affix the items to the notebook page with a permanent adhesive, such as white glue or non-yellowing transparent tape.

If you have to draw a sketch in pencil and want to make a permanent record of it (to put in your notebook) without redrawing the sketch in ink, simply make a photocopy of the penciled sketch: voila´—a permanent copy!

Finally, if there are more than two inventors, make a new space for each additional inventor to sign.

Choose witnesses who are as impartial and competent as possible, which means that ideally they should not be close relatives or people who have been working so closely with you as to be possible co-inventors. Witnesses should also be people who are likely to be available to testify later, should a dispute over your inventorship arise.

A1 RECORD YOUR CONCEPTION

■ RECOMMENDED READING—*Patent It Yourself,* Chapter 3

There are many reasons to accurately record the date and surrounding circumstances of your original conception of your invention. The most important of these is to have proof that you are the true inventor in case another inventor claims prior inventorship. Recording your conception in the manner we suggest here is like giving your invention a pedigree. With proper records, your invention will be recognized as yours; without this documentary evidence, your invention's special identity and origins are subject to challenge.

There are a number of elements involved in recording the conception of your invention. These are:

• Your invention's title;

• The circumstances of its conception;

• Its purpose or the problem solved;

• A brief functional and structural description of the invention as you have conceived it[1];

• An informal sketch;

• All of your invention's possible applications (ramifications) ;

• Your invention's novel features, insofar as you know them now;

• A brief description of the closest known prior art; and

• The advantages of the invention over previous developments and/or knowledge in the relevant field.

We can't overemphasize the importance of accurately documenting the conception of your invention, which is summed up in this Inventor's Commandment from *Patent It Yourself.*

---

[1] Space for a more detailed functional and structural description of your invention (i.e., the description of the building and testing phase) is provided in Section A2.

INVENTOR'S COMMANDMENT

After conceiving of your invention, you should not proceed to develop, build, or test it, or reveal it to outsiders until you first:

1. make a clear description of your conception;

2. sign and date the same;

3. have this document signed and dated by two people you trust to the effect that they have "witnessed and understood" your creation; and

4. 1) try to build and test your invention (if at all possible) as soon as you can, 2) keep full and true written, signed, and dated records of all the efforts, correspondence and receipts concerning your invention, especially if you build and test it, and 3) have two others sign and date that they have "witnessed and understood" your building and testing.

Following this commandment will help you:

• prove prior conception in case of an interference or theft of your idea;

• establish your inventorship in case someone else claims inventorship; and

• antedate any prior art[2] which may be cited by the Patent and Trademark Office (PTO) that may cast doubt on the originality of your invention.

If you use no other part of this notebook, we urge you to provide the documentation we suggest here. When filling out this form, remember our instructions for making entries set out in the introduction to this part. If you need more space and use the continuation pages in Part E, enter the page number on which you have continued your entry in the space provided at the bottom of page 4.

Note: You should only use this form when you have arrived at a relatively firm idea of what your invention consists of. Then, if you change your approach or think of additional complications after you have recorded your conception but prior to your building and testing activity, put these new ideas on the blank pages provided for this specific purpose (Additional Conceptions and Ramifications).

Here now is a sample recordation of the conception of an invention.

---

[2]A prior art reference is any previous patent, article, or other document or actual public knowledge or use which is relevant to the PTO's decision on whether your invention deserves a patent.

Title of invention: "Orange Peeling Knife" or "Knife that can score oranges through skin without cutting pulp."

Circumstances of conception: On March 2 or 3 of this year, when visiting my sister Shirley Goldberger in Lancaster, PA, I decided to eat an orange just before we all went shopping. When I tried to score through the orange's skin to peel it, I cut too deeply, and the orange dripped onto my lap. It stained my new pants and embarrassed me in front of Shirley, my wife, and my mother. I had to change my pants, delaying everyone in the process.

I recall telling everyone, after we eventually got going and were in the car, that there must be a better way to score and peel oranges. The problem preoccupied me so much that I didn't go shopping; instead, I came up with a solution while waiting in my car for my family. I remember telling them, on the way back, "Why not make a knife with an adjustable blade stop so that the depth of the cut could be controlled? That way you wouldn't cut into the orange's pulp, it would be easier to peel and it wouldn't drip."

I didn't make any record of the invention at that time since I didn't know I should until I read this book yesterday.

Purpose or problem solved: To peel oranges (or grapefruits or pomellos), it is desirable to score them first, preferably with two encircling cuts that cross at the blossom and stem ends so that the skin can be neatly peeled off in quarters. However, this is difficult with an ordinary knife because one inevitably cuts past the skin into the pulp, making the orange drip and the peel difficult to remove without removing some of the pulp with it. The problem is compounded because the thickness of orange peels varies among varieties. A tool that could neatly score oranges with peels of various thicknesses without cutting into the pulp would solve the problem.

Invented by: ___Edward R. Furman___   Date: _July 23, 198_
Invented by: _____   Date: _____
Witnessed and understood by: _Ruben Santiago_   Date: _July 23, 198_
Witnessed and understood by: _____   Date: _____

24

Description and operation:

My knife will have a handle and blade similar to those on a conventional paring knife. Attached to each side of the blade, however, will be a strip of plastic or wood that will serve as a stop or fence to control the depth of cuts that can be made with the knife. These fences will be moveable, allowing the depth of the cut to be varied by adjustments made to a thumbscrew that will be attached to the two fences. For thin-skinned oranges, the fences will be adjusted to permit a shallow cut, and for thick-skinned oranges, the fences will be adjusted to allow a deeper cut. In either case, the knife will easily be used to score through the skin completely around the orange without cutting deeper than the distance from the edge of the blade to the fences, and thus without cutting its pulp.

Invented by: _Edward R. Furman_   Date: _July 23, 198_

Invented by: _____   Date: _____

Witnessed and understood by: _Ruben Santiago_   Date: _July 23, 198_

Witnessed and understood by: _____   Date: _____

Drawing:

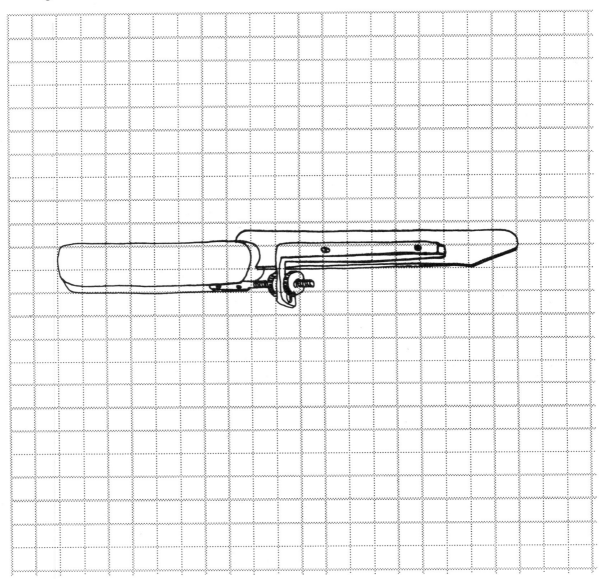

For further description, see continuation page _____.

Invented by: _Edward R. Furman_	Date: _July 23, 198_	
Invented by: _____	Date: _____	
Witnessed and understood by: _Ruben Santiago_	Date: _July 23, 198_	
Witnessed and understood by: _____	Date: _____	

26

Ramifications: _Instead of adjustable stop strips on both sides of the blade, a fixed stop strip, on one or both sides, can be used. This fixed stop strip can be mounted parallel to the edge, or it can even be inclined to the edge so that the depth of cut can be controlled by changing the longitudinal part of the blade that contacts the orange._

Novel features: _I have never seen or heard of any knife with a depth-of-cut controlling stop strip, much less an adjustable one._

Closest known prior art: _I have seen orange peelers comprising a curved knife, a curved metal rod that is inserted under the peel to move it around and free the peel from the pulp, and of course conventional paring knives._

Advantages of my invention: _My knife is the only one that can cut through an orange's peel to any desired depth. It makes peeling an orange neater, safer, and faster. All one has to do is score around the skin with two encircling cuts and then peel off the four quarter peels, leaving a peeled orange that is ready to segment and eat. Cf. the messy and difficult-to-use prior-art methods, which involve cutting the orange in quarters and peeling off the pulp, or awkward knives and tools that required skill to use and are not nearly as fast, neat and easy to use as mine._

For further description, see continuation page _____.

Invented by: _Edward R. Furman_		Date: _July 23, 198_
Invented by:		Date:
Witnessed and understood by: _Ruben Santiago_		Date: _July 23, 198_
Witnessed and understood by:		Date:

Record of Conception of Invention

Title of invention: _____

_____

_____

Circumstances of conception: _____

_____

_____

_____

_____

_____

_____

_____

_____

_____

_____

_____

_____

_____

_____

_____

Purpose or problem solved: _____

_____

_____

_____

_____

_____

_____

Invented by: _____ Date: _____

Invented by: _____ Date: _____

Witnessed and understood by: _____ Date: _____

Witnessed and understood by: _____ Date: _____

Record of Conception of Invention

Description and operation:

_____
_____
_____
_____
_____
_____
_____
_____
_____
_____
_____
_____
_____
_____
_____
_____
_____
_____
_____
_____
_____
_____
_____
_____
_____
_____
_____
_____

Invented by: _____ Date: _____

Invented by: _____ Date: _____

Witnessed and understood by: _____ Date: _____

Witnessed and understood by: _____ Date: _____

Record of Conception of Invention

Drawing:

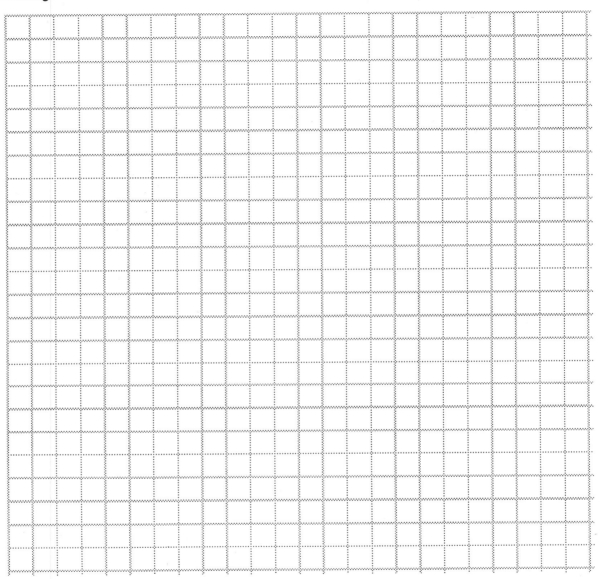

For further description, see continuation page _____.

Invented by: _____ Date: _____

Invented by: _____ Date: _____

Witnessed and understood by: _____ Date: _____

Witnessed and understood by: _____ Date: _____

Record of Conception of Invention

Ramifications: _____
_____
_____
_____
_____

Novel features: _____
_____
_____
_____
_____

Closest known prior art: _____
_____
_____
_____

Advantages of my invention: _____
_____
_____
_____
_____
_____
_____
_____
_____

For further description, see continuation page _____.

Invented by: _____ Date: _____

Invented by: _____ Date: _____

Witnessed and understood by: _____ Date: _____

Witnessed and understood by: _____ Date: _____

Additional conceptions and ramifications:

_____
_____
_____
_____
_____
_____
_____
_____
_____
_____
_____
_____
_____
_____
_____
_____
_____
_____
_____
_____
_____
_____
_____
_____
_____
_____
_____
_____
_____
_____
_____
_____
_____

Invented by: _____   Date: _____

Invented by: _____   Date: _____

Witnessed and understood by: _____   Date: _____

Witnessed and understood by: _____   Date: _____

Additional conceptions and ramifications:

_____
_____
_____
_____
_____
_____
_____
_____
_____
_____
_____
_____
_____
_____
_____
_____
_____
_____
_____
_____
_____
_____
_____
_____
_____
_____
_____
_____

Invented by: _____   Date: _____

Invented by: _____   Date: _____

Witnessed and understood by: _____   Date: _____

Witnessed and understood by: _____   Date: _____

A2 RECORD THE BUILDING AND TESTING OF YOUR INVENTION

■ RECOMMENDED READING—*Patent It Yourself,* Chapter 3

INVENTOR'S COMMANDMENT

(1) Try to build and test your invention (if at all possible) as soon as you can, (2) keep full and true written, signed, and dated records of all the efforts, correspondence and receipts concerning your invention, especially if you build and test it, and (3) have two others sign and date that they have "witnessed and understood" your building and testing.

When documenting the building and testing of your invention you should record as much factual data about the process as possible. Provide conclusions only if they are supported by factual data. Items that by their nature can't be entered directly in the notebook by hand, such as formal sketches or photos should be signed, dated, and witnessed and then pasted or affixed in the notebook in proper chronological order. You should also save all of your "other paperwork" involved with the conception, building, and testing of your invention, such as loose notes, bedside notes, receipts, letters, memos, etc. These items can be very convincing as supporting evidence to a judge if you ever need to prove any of the pertinent dates related to your invention. Because of the potential importance of this documentation, do yourself a favor and provide a place to save these papers. We suggest that you paste a 6" x 9" manila envelope inside the back cover of this book or use an expansion pocket file if the papers become too voluminous.

If you build and test your invention at the same time that you conceived of it, fill out the Record of Conception (Form A1) and add a brief note indicating that you also built and tested it at the same time. Make a reference to and then complete Form A2 after you've finished Form A1.

If you can't build and test your invention yourself, many model makers, engineers, technicians, teachers, etc. are available who will be delighted to do the job for you for a fee, or for a percentage of the action. If you do use a model maker (consultant), you should take precautions to protect the confidentiality and proprietary status of your invention. There's no substitute for checking out your consultant carefully by asking for references (assuming you don't already know the consultant by reputation or referral).

In addition, have your consultant sign a copy of the Consultant's Work Agreement included in Part G. See Chapter 4(F) of *Patent It Yourself* for instructions on completing this form.

Note: When providing this documentation, remember to follow the instructions set out at the beginning of this part. If you need more space than the 8 pages provided here, use the continuation pages in Part E (enter on the last page of Form A2 the number of the page in Part E you have continued your entries on).

OPTIONALLY, FILE A PROVISIONAL PATENT APPLICATION

Suppose you don't have the facilities, skill, or time to build and test your invention and you can't file a patent application right away. In 1994 the government enacted the GATT (General Agreements On Tariffs And Trade) implementation law, which, for the first time in the U.S., enables an inventor to file (as of 1995 Jun 8) a Provisional Patent Application (PPA) as a legal alternative to building and testing the invention. Let's explore the PPA and its advantages and disadvantages.

What It Is: A PPA is a short version of a patent application which an applicant can use to establish an early filing date for a later-filed Regular Patent Application (RPA). A PPA consists of the following:

- a detailed description of the invention telling how to make and use it

- drawing(s), if necessary to understand how to make and use the invention

- a cover sheet

- a fee, and

- an SE declaration if you're an SE and want to file the PPA with an SE fee.

What it is not: For those readers already familiar with the regular patent application process (See Part B4), unlike an RPA, a PPA does not require:

- a Patent Application Declaration (PAD)

- an Information Disclosure Statement (IDS)

- claims

- an abstract and summary

- a description of the invention's background, or

- a statement of the invention's objects and advantages.

Your PPA cannot by itself result in a patent. If you don't file an RPA within a year of your PPA's filing date, your PPA will go abandoned and will be forever useless. Also, your PPA cannot provide a filing date for subject matter that is not disclosed in it.

What type of detailed description is necessary for a valid PPA?

Your PPA must disclose clearly and fully how to make and use the invention. That is, it must have the same level of detail that is required in the part of the Specification section of a regular patent application where you describe the invention's main embodiment and operation.

The PTO will not examine your PPA for compliance with this description requirement unless you later file a regular patent application (RPA) claiming the benefit of your PPA filing date and the PTO needs to verify the adequacy of the description because of conflicting prior art.

When to file a PPA: We recommend that you file a PPA only if:

- you want to establish an early filing date because you feel your invention is potentially valuable and might be independently developed by others or stolen from you

- you can't or don't want to build and test your invention now, and

- you can't or don't want to file an RPA on it now.

Additional reasons to file a PPA are:

- You can file a PPA, then, within one year, file an RPA, which has the practical effect of delaying examination of the RPA and extending—up to one year—your patent's expiration date.

- You can file an RPA, convert it to a PPA one year later, and then file a second RPA based upon the PPA to extend your patent's expiration date for two years.

Reasons you may not wish to file a PPA are:

- You may tend to forego building and testing and lose the concomitant advantages, such as determining whether the invention is operable, practical, useful and having a working prototype to demonstrate to prospective manufacturers.

- The filing fee is not insignificant (as of June 8, 1995, $75 for small entities, $150 for large entities).

- Your PPA must contain a full a description of the actual nuts and bolts of the invention, and how it will operate. Just like an RPA, absent this description, the PPA will have no legal effect.

- You cannot wait one year after filing the RPA to foreign file. Instead you must make your foreign filing decision, as well as your regular U.S. filing decision, within one year after your PPA is filed.

See Part B3 for the steps necessary to prepare a PPA

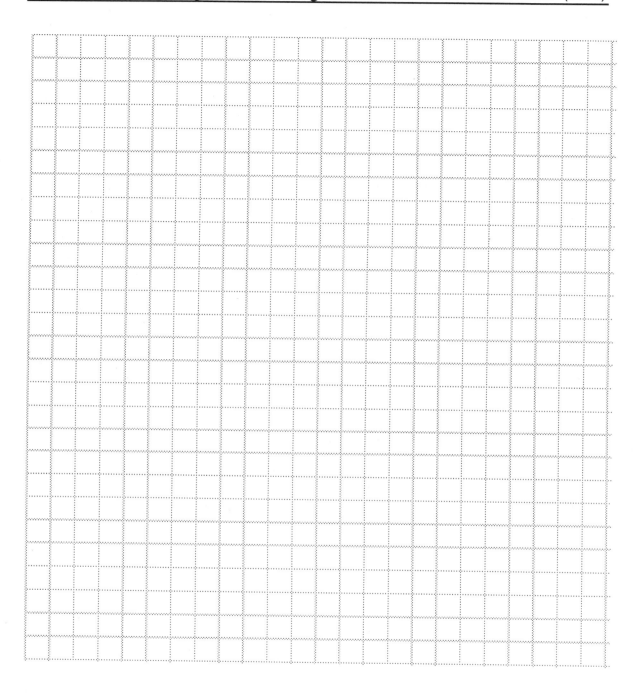

Invented by: _____   Date: _____

Invented by: _____   Date: _____

Witnessed and understood by: _____   Date: _____

Witnessed and understood by: _____   Date: _____

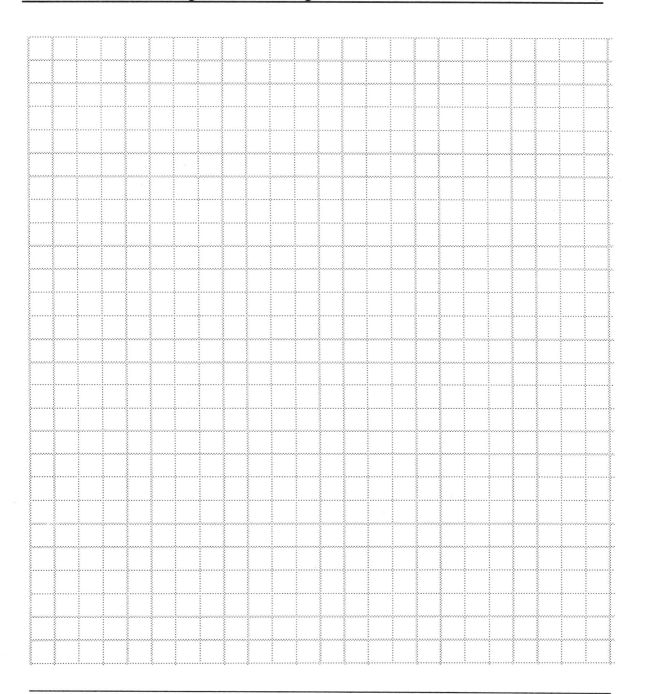

Invented by: _____   Date: _____

Invented by: _____   Date: _____

Witnessed and understood by: _____   Date: _____

Witnessed and understood by: _____   Date: _____

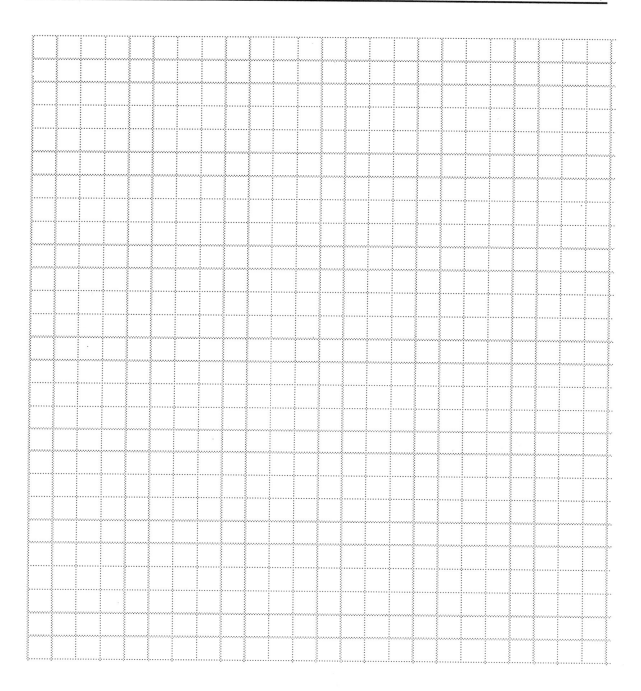

Invented by: _____ Date: _____

Invented by: _____ Date: _____

Witnessed and understood by: _____ Date: _____

Witnessed and understood by: _____ Date: _____

Invented by: _____ Date: _____

Invented by: _____ Date: _____

Witnessed and understood by: _____ Date: _____

Witnessed and understood by: _____ Date: _____

Invented by: _____   Date: _____

Invented by: _____   Date: _____

Witnessed and understood by: _____   Date: _____

Witnessed and understood by: _____   Date: _____

Invented by: _____   Date: _____

Invented by: _____   Date: _____

Witnessed and understood by: _____   Date: _____

Witnessed and understood by: _____   Date: _____

Invented by: _____ Date: _____

Invented by: _____ Date: _____

Witnessed and understood by: _____ Date: _____

Witnessed and understood by: _____ Date: _____

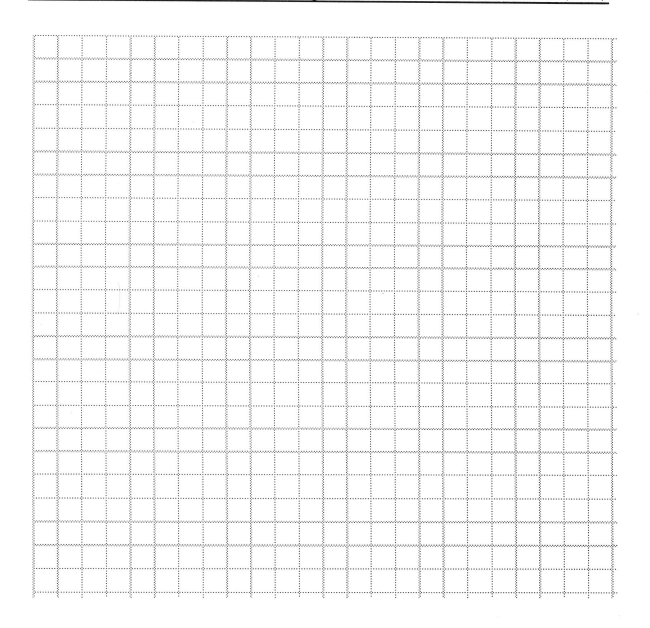

For further description, see continuation page _____.

Invented by: _____ Date: _____

Invented by: _____ Date: _____

Witnessed and understood by: _____ Date: _____

Witnessed and understood by: _____ Date: _____

A3 OTHER POSSIBLE APPLICATIONS OF YOUR INVENTION

■ RECOMMENDED READING—*Patent it Yourself,* Chapter 2

As you proceed to build and test your invention, you will probably have flashes of insight as to other possible uses for it. This section of the notebook is designed specifically for you to immediately record these "bolts from the blue" so that later on, when you draft your patent application or formulate marketing plans, you can easily refer to them.

1. Alternative application and change required:

_____
_____
_____
_____

2. Alternative application and change required:

_____
_____
_____
_____

3. Alternative application and change required:

_____
_____
_____
_____

4. Alternative application and change required:

_____
_____
_____
_____

5. Alternative application and change required:

_____
_____
_____
_____

Invented by: _____ Date: _____

Invented by: _____ Date: _____

Witnessed and understood by: _____ Date: _____

Witnessed and understood by: _____ Date: _____

A4 RECORD YOUR TRADEMARK CONCEPTION

■ RECOMMENDED READING—*Patent It Yourself,* Chapter 1

The brand name or design symbol (or both) that you attach to or associate with your invention for marketing purposes is known as a trademark. Needless to say, if your product is successful in the marketplace your trademark can become very valuable. This form is provided for recording a drawing or description of any trademark you create. We provide space for four trademark conceptions in case a trademark search reveals a conflict.

For each trademark you should provide the mark itself (a name, graphic design, or a name with a graphic design together with the generic descriptor ("goods" or service) with which the mark is to be used. E. g., with IVORY soap, "IVORY" is the mark and "soap" is the goods or generic descriptor.

Note: Although your proposed trademark will not be subject to protection under federal and state trademark laws until you either use it, or apply to register it on the basis of intended use, it can be considered a trade secret until that time. Accordingly, we suggest these pages be signed, dated and witnessed so you can prove that you came up with the name first in case of a trade secret dispute on this point. In Section B5 you can record details as to the use and registration of your trademark in case of a later dispute over its ownership.

Distinctive Name/Design & Goods/Service:

Distinctive Name/Design & Goods/Service:

Conceived by:		Date:
Conceived by:		Date:
Witnessed and understood by:		Date:
Witnessed and understood by:		Date:

Distinctive Name/Design & Goods/Service:

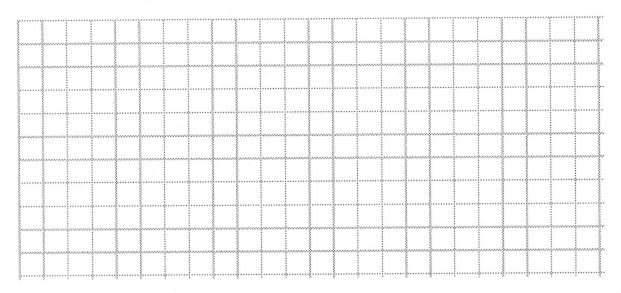

Distinctive Name/Design & Goods/Service:

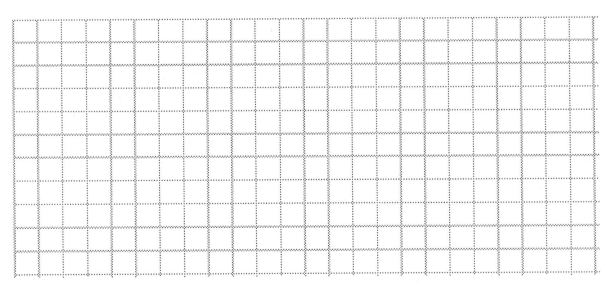

Conceived by:_____ Date:_____

Conceived by:_____ Date:_____

Witnessed and understood by: _____ Date:_____

Witnessed and understood by: _____ Date:_____

A5 RECORD YOUR DISTINCTIVE DESIGN CONCEPTION

■ RECOMMENDED READING—*Patent It Yourself,* Chapter 1

In this part of your notebook, you should enter any distinctive product designs you feel might qualify for either copyright or design patent protection. By product design, we mean the shape of your invention, such as the shape of a computer case, the shape of a bottle, the design of jewelry, etc. We provide four pages for you to do this. You should record the conception and the building and testing of your design, just as you did for a utility invention. If, however, your design is already shown in the conception (A1) or building and testing (A2) documentation of your utility invention, then of course that will suffice and you don't have to make separate documentation records for the design.

If your invention has a distinctive design that is basically unrelated to its function, you may be able to protect the design from use by others by a design patent or copyright.

Design patents last for 14 years and give you the right to prevent others from using your distinctive design for that period of time, even if they created the design independently of you.[3] Copyright protection is useable for designs of toys and nonutilitarian articles, such as jewelry, or even utilitarian articles where the artwork is separable from the article, such as fabric design. Copyright protection lasts for your life plus 50 years (or for 75-100 years if the design was created as a work made for hire) and gives you the right to exclude others from copying your work. Each form of protection has some advantages and disadvantages. The primary advantage of the design patent is that it offers a broader scope of protection. The copyright, on the other hand, is much easier to create and maintain, and offers

---

[3]How to get a design patent is discussed in Chapter 10 of *Patent It Yourself.*

protection for a longer period of time.[4] Because of the greater value of its advantages, we recommend that you use copyright protection for all toys, nonutilitarian articles and objects. If the object is utilitarian and its aesthetic features can't be separated from the article, use design patent protection.

---

[4]We recommend that you not try to obtain both forms of protection for one design. Asserting two "monopolies" over one creation may be construed by the courts as overreaching and may therefore result in a loss of protection for your design.

Drawing(s)

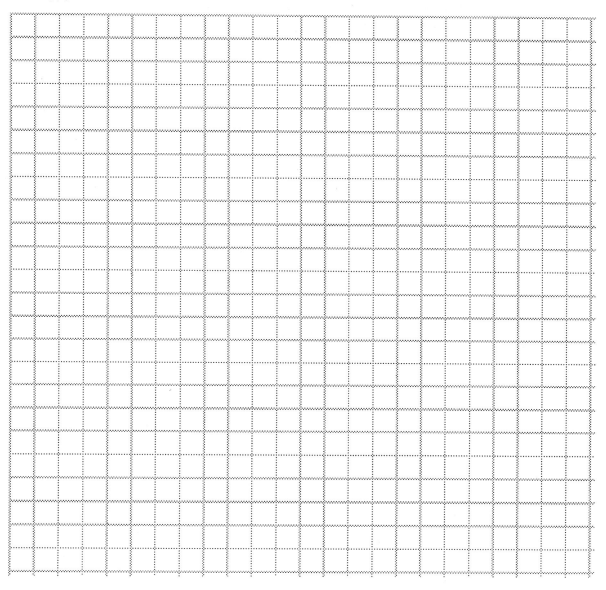

Invented by: _____ Date: _____

Invented by: _____ Date: _____

Witnessed and understood by: _____ Date: _____

Witnessed and understood by: _____ Date: _____

Drawing(s)

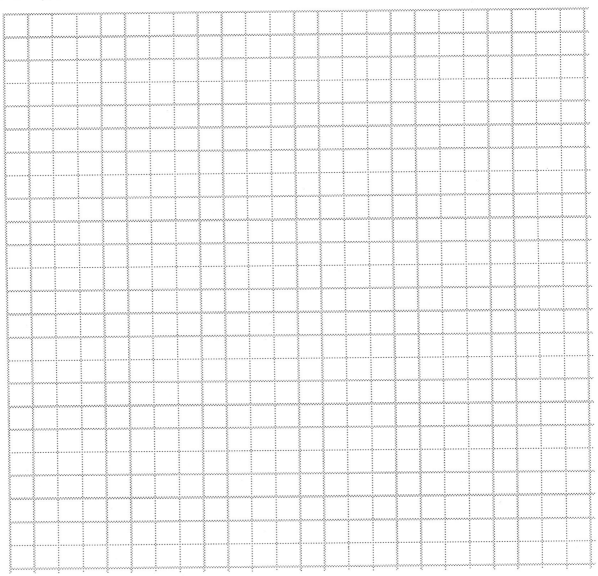

Invented by: _____ Date: _____

Invented by: _____ Date: _____

Witnessed and understood by: _____ Date: _____

Witnessed and understood by: _____ Date: _____

Drawing(s)

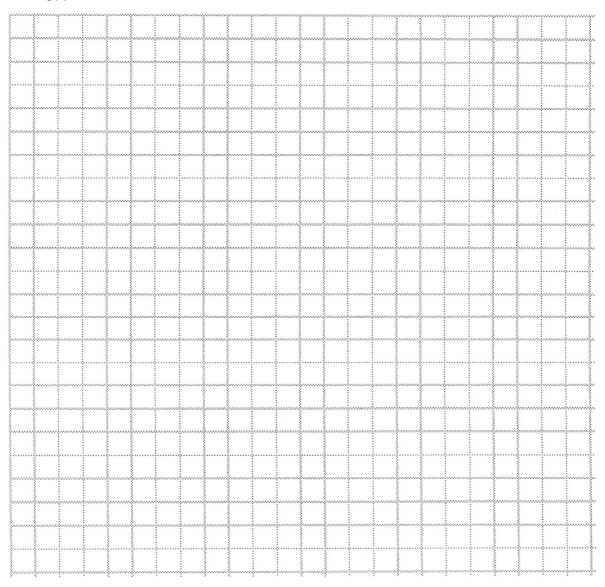

Invented by: _____ Date: _____

Invented by: _____ Date: _____

Witnessed and understood by: _____ Date: _____

Witnessed and understood by: _____ Date: _____

Drawing(s)

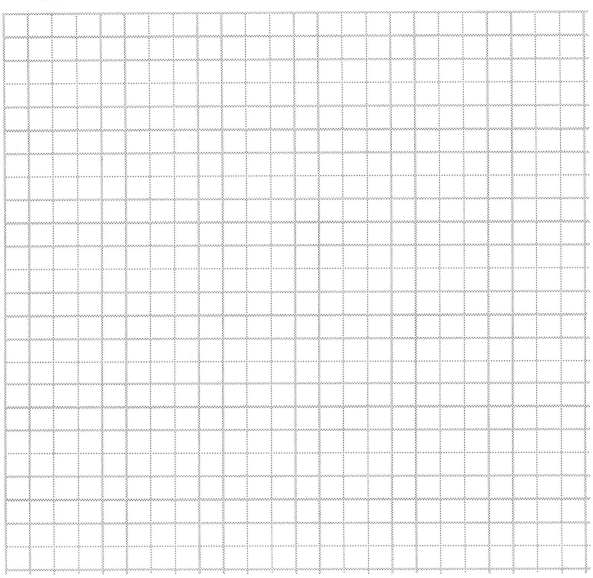

Invented by:	Date:
Invented by:	Date:
Witnessed and understood by:	Date:
Witnessed and understood by:	Date:

PART B

Legal Protection

Part B: Legal Protection

This part of *The Inventor's Notebook* helps you organize and record the information you will need to obtain the fullest possible legal protection for your invention. It is divided into the following six sections:

• Section B1 (Prior Art Search) helps you keep track of the prior art which will ultimately determine whether your invention receives a patent (and which you must disclose to the PTO as part of you patent application). This section also alerts you to any public use or exposure of your invention which might trigger the rule requiring filing of a patent application within one year of such public use or exposure.

• Section B2 (Patentability Checklist) provides a form which will help you assess the patentability of your invention.

• Section B3 (Patent Application Checklist) contains a patent application checklist which helps you keep track of the many items and steps involved in preparing and filing a complete patent application.

• Section B4 (Design Patent Application Checklist) helps you organize your effort to obtain a design patent.

- Section B5 (Trademark Use and Registration) is where you document the results of any trademark search you have conducted regarding your proposed trademark for your invention, the first use (if any) of the trademark, and information about steps you have taken to protect the trademark (registration and renewal with the PTO and state agencies).

- Section B6 (Record of Contacts) allows you to record all contacts you make with outside individuals and companies about your invention, and whether you have obtained confidentiality agreements (we call them Proprietary Material Loan Agreements) as appropriate. This information will help you maintain your invention as a trade secret pending the issuance of a patent.

- Section B7 (Legal Protection Summary) is a checklist which lets you know whether you have done what you should to legally protect your invention and trademark.

B1 PRIOR ART SEARCH

■ RECOMMENDED READING—*Patent It Yourself,* Chapter 6

INVENTOR'S COMMANDMENT

You should make (or have made) a thorough patentability search of your invention before you file a patent application.

Is your invention patentable (Box 16)? This section of the notebook is where you enter the information which will help you answer this question. As you probably know, whether your invention is patentable depends in large part upon previous developments in the same field (prior art). Most specialized inventors have a good working grasp of the relevant prior art and are able to come up with something different, at least to some degree.[1] Awareness of this prior art usually comes from:

• reviewing previously issued patents;

• researching trade journal articles; and

• carefully checking wholesale and retail channels to see whether a similar product has been marketed.

It is important for you to conduct a preliminary search of relevant prior art to determine whether your invention is sufficiently innovative to qualify for a patent. Keep careful track of the prior art references you accumulate in the course of your preliminary search. This is because later, when you file your patent application, you will need to designate all prior art known to you. Documenting all prior art you discover as you go along will make your actual patent application process a whole lot easier.

---

[1] Of course most inventors invent first and then check to see whether it qualifies for a patent.

This section also asks you to document the date your Invention is first exposed to or used in public in a way that might trigger the one-year rule.

INVENTOR'S COMMANDMENT

One-Year Rule: You should treat the "one-year rule" as holy. You must file your patent application within one year of the date on which you first publish, publicly use, sell, or offer your invention, or any product which embodies same, for sale. Moreover if you wish to preserve your foreign rights and frustrate pirates of your creation, you should actually file your patent application before you publish or sell your creation.

STEPS   DATE

1. My earliest provable date of invention:

   _____   _____

   _____   _____

2. Date of the first public use, offer for sale, public disclosure or commercial disclosure of my invention:

   _____   _____

   _____   _____

3. Publications searched:
   a. _____   _____
   b. _____   _____
   c. _____   _____
   d. _____   _____
   e. _____   _____
   f. _____   _____
   g. _____   _____

4. Search of similar products (include stores visited):
   a. _____   _____

   _____

   b. _____   _____

   _____

   c. _____   _____

   _____

   d. _____   _____

   _____

   e. _____   _____

   _____

   f. _____   _____

   _____

   g. _____   _____

   _____

STEPS   DATE

5. Patent search

    Prior relevant U.S. patents discovered (include patent numbers
    and patent class)

    a. _____   _____

    _____

    b. _____   _____

    _____

    c. _____   _____

    _____

    d. _____   _____

    _____

    e. _____   _____

    _____

    f. _____   _____

    _____

    g. _____   _____

    _____

    h. _____   _____

    _____

    i. _____   _____

    _____

    j. _____   _____

    _____

    k. _____   _____

    _____

    l. _____   _____

    _____

    m. _____   _____

    _____

    n. _____   _____

    _____

B2 PATENTABILITY CHECKLIST

■ RECOMMENDED READING—*Patent It Yourself,* Chapter 5

This section of the Notebook is where you put your reasons why you believe your invention is patentable. To be patentable, an invention must:

• fit within one of the statutory classes of patentable inventions;

• be useful;

• be novel; and

• be unobvious from the standpoint of one skilled in the relevant art.

By filling out the following form you will gain a preliminary understanding of whether your invention is patentable or whether any alternate form of legal protection should be sought. We provide three copies, as it is possible that you will come up with a number of versions of your invention in the course of prosecuting your patent application in the Patent and Trademark Office.

My invention is a new and useful[2]:

☐   Process or method

☐   Machine (includes electrical circuits)

☐   Article of manufacture

☐   Composition of matterr (includes new life forms)

☐   New use of one of the above

THESE NOVEL PHYSICAL FEATURES[3]   *PRODUCE*   THESE NEW UNEXPECTED RESULTS

a.   a.

b.   b.

c.   c.

d.   d.

---

[2]It doesn't matter what category you can subsume your invention, as long as you can fit it into one or more of these categories. They do overlap to some extent.

[3]Remember that a novel physical feature can be a novel combination of old physical features.

Patentability Checklist

My invention is a new and useful

☐ Process or method

☐ Machine (includes electrical circuits)

☐ Article of manufacture

☐ Composition of matterr (includes new life forms)

☐ New use of one of the above

THESE NOVEL PHYSICAL FEATURES	*PRODUCE*	THESE NEW UNEXPECTED RESULTS
a.		a.
b.		b.
c.		c.
d.		d.

My invention is a new and useful:

☐ Process or method

☐ Machine (includes electrical circuits)

☐ Article of manufacture

☐ Composition of matterr (includes new life forms)

☐ New use of one of the above

THESE NOVEL PHYSICAL FEATURES   *PRODUCE*   THESE NEW UNEXPECTED RESULTS

a.   a.

b.   b.

c.   c.

d.   d.

B3 PROVISIONAL PATENT APPLICATION CHECKLIST

■ RECOMMENDED READING—*Patent It Yourself,* Chapters 3, 8

Below is a list of the basic components that make up a Provisional Patent Application (PPA). Check off each step of the process as it is completed. Remember: the PPA won't do you any good unless you adequately describe your invention in it (see Part A2 for more on this requirement) and then file a regular patent application within one year. Also remember that your PPA filing date begins the one-year period you have to accomplish most foreign filings. See Chapter 3 of *Patent It Yourself* for specific filing instructions, and Chapter 8 of *Patent It Yourself* for instructions on how to adequately describe the structure and operation of your invention.

_____ 1. prepare drawings, if necessary

_____ 2. describe invention

_____ 3. describe operation

_____ 4. prepare a cover letter

_____ 5. prepare any needed small-entity declarations

_____ 6. attach a check for the filing fee and a postcard

_____ 7. mail all papers to the PTO

B4 PATENT APPLICATION CHECKLIST

■ RECOMMENDED READING—*Patent It Yourself,* Chapters 8, 13, 15

> ### INVENTOR'S COMMANDMENT
>
> Your patent application must contain a description of your invention in such full, complete, clear, and exact terms, including details of your preferred embodiment at the time you file, so that anyone having ordinary skill in the field will be readily able to make and use it, and preferably so that even a lay judge will be able to understand it.

Here is a list of the basic components which make up a patent application. When you think you are ready to file your patent application, you will want to consult this list and see whether in fact you are ready to fulfill the requirements of each component. You should also check off (in the space provided) each step of the patent process as it is completed. This will help you know exactly where you stand in respect to your application as a whole.

After your patent application has been submitted, there will be additional transactions with the PTO. We also provide a checklist for the most common of these transactions.

DATE

A. APPLICATION   _____

_____ 1. Self-addressed receipt postcard

_____ 2. Transmittal letter

_____ 3. Check for filing fee

_____ 4. Formal drawings

_____ 5. Specification:

      _____ a. Title

      _____ b. Cross references to corresponding applications

      _____ c. Background—Field of invention

      _____ d. Background—Discussion of prior art

      _____ e. Objects and advantages

      _____ f. Description of drawings

      _____ g. List of drawing reference numerals

      _____ h. Summary

      _____ i. Description of invention

      _____ j. Operation of invention

      _____ k. Conclusions, ramifications, scope

_____ 6. Claims

_____ 7. Abstract

_____ 8. Completed Declaration Form

_____ 9. Small Entity Declaration

_____ 10. Information Disclosure Statement and List of Prior Art Cited   _____

_____ 11. Assignment and Assignment Cover Sheet

DATE

_____

B. AMENDMENT

_____1._   All pages completed?

_____2._   All points in Office Action answered?

_____3._   If number of claims is increased, is any necessary additional fee enclosed?

_____4._   Is Certificate of Mailing included?

_____5._   Is Amendment mailed on time or Petition to Extend with fee included?

_____6._   If Petition to Extend is included, is it properly completed with proper fee?

_____7._   Amendment signed and dated by proper party(ies)?

_____8._   Envelope properly addressed and stamped?

_____9._   Is stamped, addressed, properly completed return postcard enclosed?

_____10._   Enough file copies made?

C. PAYING ISSUE FEE

_____

_____1._   Issue Fee Transmittal form filled out and signed?

_____2._   Check for correct amount attached and signed?

_____3._   Postcard attached, stamped, addressed?

_____4._   Any needed drawing corrections attended to?

_____5._   Certificate of Mailing attached, completed, signed, dated?

_____6._   Mailed on time? (Three month period is not extendable.)

_____7._   Is stamped, addressed, properly completed return postcard enclosed?

_____8._   Enough file copies made?

B5 DESIGN PATENT APPLICATION CHECKLIST

■ RECOMMENDED READING—*Patent It Yourself,* Chapter 10

Here is a list of the components which go into a design patent application. If you decided that a separate design patent is appropriate for your invention, you will want to consult this list and see whether you are ready to file. Again, check off each step as you complete it so that you can help keep track of where you are.

Design Patent Application Checklist

DATE

___1.___   Design Patent Application   _____

___2.___   The Drawing(s)   _____

___3.___   Patent Application Declaration   _____

___4.___   Small Entity Declaration   _____

___5.___   Filing Fee   _____

___6.___   Receipt Postcard   _____

___7.___   Information Disclosure Statement and List of Prior Art Cited   _____

B6 TRADEMARK USE AND REGISTRATION

In Part A4 of this notebook we ask you to describe the trademark you plan to market your invention under (if any). In this part we provide forms for you to document the steps you should take to make sure this trademark is valid and cannot be used by competitors.[4]

The first step is to determine whether your proposed trademark is sufficiently distinguishable from existing trademarks to avoid later charges of trademark infringement. This effort (termed a trademark search) usually involves, at a minimum, an examination of:

- the list of trademarks registered (and pending registrations) with the Patent and Trademark Office;

- the list of trademarks registered in your state;

- existing product and service names (trademarks and service marks); and

- trade and product journals covering subjects related to your invention.

Although it is possible to conduct your own trademark search, the more common practice is to have a professional trademark searcher do it (at a cost of between $100 and $250 per trademark searched). The name of your searcher and the sources searches (either by your searcher or by you if you did the search yourself) should be entered in the space provided.

The criteria for determining the extent to which you can prevent others from using your trademark, and whether it infringes other existing trademarks, are discussed briefly in Chapter 1 of *Patent It Yourself.* You should consult a trademark attorney if you have any doubts about either or both of these points.

Once you decide on a trademark, you should file an application to register your trademark on the basis of your good faith intent to use it within the following six months. Then, when the trademark is actually used to market your invention across state lines, you can file an Amendment to Allege Use to get the trademark placed on the federal trademark register. If you are already using a trademark across state lines, your registration would be based on actual rather than intended use.

If you see that you won't be able to actually use the mark across state lines within the six month period, you can obtain a six month extension upon a showing of good cause. Four additional six-month extensions can also be obtained if you are able to convince the PTO that you still have a good faith intent to use the mark.

---

[4] For more information on all aspects of trademark law and instructions on how to register a trademark, see *Trademark: How To Name a Business and Product,* by Kate McGrath & Stephen Elias (Nolo Press).

Under this system, you initially have several dates to keep track of:

- the date you first use your work within a state;

- the date you file your trademark application to register on basis of intended use;

- the date you put the trademark into actual use across state lines; and

- the date you file your Amendment to Allege Use (or alternatively, your Statement of Use, if the PTO has by then issued the Notice of Allowance provisionally registering your mark).

You should also document when you first used the trademark in a foreign country as this may be important should your trademark go international.

Your PTO registration provides notice throughout the U.S. that you claim ownership of and have the exclusive right to use the mark for the goods indicated in the registration. This notice can often make the difference between stopping other people from using your trademark and having to share use of the trademark with these later users. Also, it is much easier to collect damages for infringement of a registered trademark than an unregistered one. Use the space provided to document your federal registration efforts, including the date of registration, registration number, and registration classification name and number (all trademarks fall into one or more specific classes of goods, each of which is assigned a number).

When your trademark is registered, you should note the date when you will need to file your declarations of continued use and incontestability[5] (within the last year of the six year period after your initial registration date). Thus, if you register your trademark with the PTO on July 1 1991, you will want to file these declarations between July 1, 1996 and July 1, 1997. You should also note the date you will want to initiate your ten-year renewal (about six months before the end of the ten-year period following your registration).

Caution: The protection and proper use of a trademark can be as commercially important as the underlying invention. We strongly recommend that you get a copy of *Trademark: How To Name a Business & Product,* by Kate McGrath and Stephen Elias (Nolo Press) and, if necessary, work with a trademark attorney on the matters covered in this part of *The Inventor's Notebook.*

---

[5]These are statements that your trademark has been in continuous use for the preceding five year period and that you qualify to have made your trademark made incontestable (which immunizes it from attack on certain grounds). Failure to file the declaration of continued use will result in your trademark being cancelled. Assuming you are working with a trademark attorney, he or she will keep the date these declarations are due on the law firm calendar.

STEPS   DATE

1. Final version of trademark conceived   _____
    (documented in Section A4)

2. Trademark search completed   _____

    a. Name of searcher

        _____

    b. Federally registered trademarks   _____

    c. State registered trademarks   _____

    d. Trade journals and product lists
        (1) _____
        (2) _____
        (3) _____
        (4) _____
        (5) _____
        (6) _____
        (7) _____
        (8) _____

3. First use of trademark

    a   Intrastate   _____

    a. Interstate   _____

    b. Foreign   _____

STEPS

4. Registration of trademark with PTO*

   a. Date regular application filed (trademark already in use)　　　_____

   b. Date application based upon intent to use filed　　　_____

   c. Date Amendment to Allege Use filed　　　_____

   d. Date registration granted　　　_____

   e. Registration #　　　_____

   f. _____ Principal Register　　　_____ Supplemental Register

   g. Class and description of goods:

   _____

   _____

   _____

5. Renewal of federal registration

   a. §§ 8/15 Declarations due by　　　_____

   b. Renewal due by　　　_____

*State trademark registration also exists. If you aren't using your invention across states, consider placing it on your state's trademark register.

B7   RECORD OF CONTACTS

■ RECOMMENDED READING—*Patent It Yourself,* Chapter 1

It is extremely important that an inventor be able to identify each and every person and company who has been contacted about, or had access to, the invention. This information can prove to be very useful in the event of a dispute about:

• the inventor's diligence in building and testing the invention;

• who should be considered the true inventor; or

• whether a confidentiality agreement has been violated.[6]

Also, you will need to call some of those people again, and it will be helpful if you have a record of what you discussed the last time and what their response was. By conscientiously entering all contacts in this section of the notebook, and noting whether the person contacted has signed a confidentiality agreement, you will have all your contacts and trade secret protection information collected in one place for later reference.

---

[6]Once a patent issues on your invention, it becomes a matter of public record. Prior to obtaining a patent, however, you are entitled to treat your invention as a trade secret and obtain court relief against those who improperly disclose your invention to others. Generally, a trade secret is any information which is maintained as confidential and which, because it is not generally known to competitors, provides its owner with a competitive edge. The basic method for preserving information as a trade secret is to limit those who have access to it, and require those who do have access to sign a confidentiality agreement. Blank agreement forms (called Proprietary Materials Agreements) are located in Part G.

Record of Contacts

NAME & TITLE   DATE   AGREEMENT SIGNED?

_____   _____   _____

Address & Phone: _____

_____

_____

Comments: _____

_____

_____

Follow up? _____

_____

NAME & TITLE   DATE   AGREEMENT SIGNED?

_____   _____   _____

Address & Phone: _____

_____

_____

Comments: _____

_____

_____

Follow up? _____

_____

NAME & TITLE   DATE   AGREEMENT SIGNED?

_____   _____   _____

Address & Phone: _____

_____

_____

Comments: _____

_____

_____

Follow up? _____

_____

Record of Contacts

NAME & TITLE   DATE   AGREEMENT SIGNED?

_____   _____   _____

Address & Phone: _____

_____

_____

Comments: _____

_____

_____

Follow up? _____

_____

NAME & TITLE   DATE   AGREEMENT SIGNED?

_____   _____   _____

Address & Phone: _____

_____

_____

Comments: _____

_____

_____

Follow up? _____

_____

NAME & TITLE   DATE   AGREEMENT SIGNED?

_____   _____   _____

Address & Phone: _____

_____

_____

Comments: _____

_____

_____

Follow up? _____

_____

NAME & TITLE   DATE   AGREEMENT SIGNED?
_____   _____   _____

Address & Phone: _____
_____
_____

Comments: _____
_____
_____

Follow up? _____
_____

NAME & TITLE   DATE   AGREEMENT SIGNED?
_____   _____   _____

Address & Phone: _____
_____
_____

Comments: _____
_____
_____

Follow up? _____
_____

NAME & TITLE   DATE   AGREEMENT SIGNED?
_____   _____   _____

Address & Phone: _____
_____
_____

Comments: _____
_____
_____

Follow up? _____
_____

Record of Contacts

NAME & TITLE   DATE   AGREEMENT SIGNED?

_____   _____   _____

Address & Phone: _____

_____

_____

Comments: _____

_____

_____

Follow up? _____

_____

NAME & TITLE   DATE   AGREEMENT SIGNED?

_____   _____   _____

Address & Phone: _____

_____

_____

Comments: _____

_____

_____

Follow up? _____

_____

NAME & TITLE   DATE   AGREEMENT SIGNED?

_____   _____   _____

Address & Phone: _____

_____

_____

Comments: _____

_____

_____

Follow up? _____

_____

Record of Contacts

NAME & TITLE   DATE   AGREEMENT SIGNED?

_____   _____   _____

Address & Phone: _____

                  _____

                  _____

Comments: _____

           _____

           _____

Follow up? _____

            _____

NAME & TITLE   DATE   AGREEMENT SIGNED?

_____   _____   _____

Address & Phone: _____

                  _____

                  _____

Comments: _____

           _____

           _____

Follow up? _____

            _____

NAME & TITLE   DATE   AGREEMENT SIGNED?

_____   _____   _____

Address & Phone: _____

                  _____

                  _____

Comments: _____

           _____

           _____

Follow up? _____

            _____

B8 LEGAL PROTECTION SUMMARY

■ RECOMMENDED READING—*Patent It Yourself*, Chapter 7

An analysis of the relative advantages and disadvantages of the legal protection alternatives open to an inventor is provided in Chapter 7 of *Patent It Yourself.* You will want to keep track of which methods you have chosen. This listing can be very important when you go to market your invention. Most prospective buyers or developers will first want to know exactly what you've done to protect your right to exclusive use of the invention. By conscientiously keeping this list up to date, your record of protection will be instantly available to all who are interested.

MEANS OF PROTECTION   DATE

1. Conception recorded, signed, dated and witnessed   _____ date

2. Disclosure of conception signed, dated, recorded and witnessed   _____ date

3. Disclosure document filed (optional)   _____ date

4. Building and testing recorded, signed, dated, and witnessed   _____ date

5. Provisional Patent Application filed (optional)   _____ date

6. Patent application filed   _____ date

7. Patent pending notice on invention   ___ yes   ___ no

8. Patent application allowed   _____ date

9. Foreign patent application(s) filed

     a.   _____ date

     b.   _____ date

     c.   _____ date

     d.   _____ date

     e.   _____ date

10. Trade secret without patent application   ___ yes   ___ no

11. First trademark use   _____ date

12 State trademark registration   _____ date

13. Trademark registration with PTO   _____ date

14. Design patent application filed   _____ date

15. Design patent approved   _____ date

16. Copyright notice on design, artwork or written materials   ___ yes   ___ no

17. Copyright registered   _____ date

18. Sold invention before filing for patent   _____ date

PART C

Marketing

Part C: Marketing

INVENTOR'S COMMANDMENT

You should try to market your invention as soon as you can after filing your patent application; don't wait until your patent issues. You should favor companies who are close to you and small in size.

If you want your invention to be successful, pursue commercial exploitation with all the energy which you can devote to it.

Never pay any money to any invention developer unless the developer can prove to you that it has a successful track record— that is, most of its clients have received more income in royalties than they have paid the developer in fees.

Simply put, this part is a preliminary guide to help you analyze the commercial potential of your invention and to help you keep track of your efforts to market it.

Once you invent something, you will naturally want to profit from it. This will involve coming up with a plan under which your invention can be produced and distributed to its ultimate users. To effectively get your invention "out there" you need to have a handle on what its strong and weak points are from both a marketing and manufacturing point of view (Section C1). In addition, it's wise to consider how prospective manufacturers and users are likely to view your invention and to use this knowledge creatively as part of a plan to sell the idea of your new product (Section C2). It's also important to understand general market trends in the particular area of your invention so that you will be prepared to tell interested marketers and manufacturers why your invention will be profitable given the costs to make it, the competition, and so on (Section C3). In addition, you need to proceed in an organized manner to either seek potential manufacturers or distributors, or to accomplish these activities yourself. Sections C4 and C5 help you do this.

Note: The subject of marketing your invention to the public once it is manufactured is far beyond the scope of this notebook. If you plan to run the whole show, including the actual marketing of your invention, we suggest you consult one or more of the resources listed in our Bibliography in Part F.

C1 EVALUATION OF POSITIVE AND NEGATIVE FACTORS OF INVENTION

■ RECOMMENDED READING—*Patent it Yourself,* Chapter

Inventor's Commandment

You should not spend significant time or money on your creation until you have thoroughly evaluated it for commercial potential, including considering all of its advantages and disadvantages.

Before you even prepare a patent application you will obviously want to give serious consideration to whether your invention has commercial potential. For this reason, *Patent It Yourself* devotes an entire chapter to this question and provides an evaluation sheet to help you answer this key question. This same evaluation sheet has been included in this notebook in Part G (Positive/Negative Factors Evalustion). Instructions from *Patent It Yourself* have been provided for your convenience.

THE POSITIVE AND NEGATIVE FACTORS TEST

Every invention, no matter how many positive factors it seems to have at first glance, inevitably has one or more significant negative ones. To evaluate the positive and negative factors objectively, carefully consider each on the list below. Using a Positive/Negative Factors Evaluation form from Part G, assign a commercial value or disadvantage weight to each factor on a scale of 1 to 100, according to your best, carefully-considered estimate.

For example, if an invention provides overwhelming cost savings in relation to its existing counterparts, assign an 80 or higher to the "Cost" factor (#1) in the positive column. If it requires only a moderate capital expenditure (tooling) to build, a 50 would be appropriate for this factor (#43), in the negative column and so on.

The following balance scale analogy will help you understand the positive and negative factors evaluation process: pretend the positive factors are stacked on one side of a balance scale and the negative factors are stacked on the other side, as indicated below.

Cheaper Cost	Legal Problems
Lighter Weight	Operability Problems
Smaller Size	Difficult to Develop
Safer	Hard to Sell At a Profit
Etc.	Etc.
POSITIVE FACTORS	NEGATIVE FACTORS

▲

Yes	Potential Salability?	No

If the positive factors strongly outweigh the negative, you can regard this as a "go" indication, i.e., the invention is commercially viable. Obviously this balance scale is just an analogy. It can't be used quantitatively because no one has yet come up with a way to assign accurate and valid weights to the factors. Nevertheless, you'll find it of great help in evaluating the commercial prospects of your invention.

Before you actually take pen (or word processor) in hand and begin your evaluation, read through the following summary of positive and negative factors.

Positive and Negative Factors Evaluation

Inventor(s): _____   Invention: _____

_____   _____

Factor	Weight if Positive	Weight if Negative
1. Cost		
2. Weight		
3. Size		
4. Safety/Health		
5. Speed		
6. Ease of Use		
7. Ease of Production		
8. Durability		
9. Repairability		
10. Novelty		
11. Convenience/Social Benefit/Mechanization		
12. Reliability		
13. Ecology		
14. Salability		
15. Appearance		
16. Viewability		
17. Precision		
18. Noise		
19. Odor		
20. Taste		
21. Market Size		
22. Trend of Demand		
23. Seasonal Demand		
24. Difficulty of Market Penetration		
25. Potential Competition		
26. Quality		
27. Excitement		
28. Markup		

Factor	Weight if Positive	Weight if Negative
29. Inferior Performance		
30. "Sexy" Packaging		
31. Miscellaneous		
32. Long Life Cycle		
33. Related Product Addability		
34. Satisfies Existing Need		
35. Legality		
36. Operability		
37. Development		
38. Profitability		
39. Obsolescence		
40. Incompatability		
41. Product Liability Risk		
42. Market Dependence		
43. Difficulty of Distribution		
44. Service Requirements		
45. New Tooling Required		
46. Inertia Must Be Overcome		
47. Too Advanced Technically		
48. Substantial Learning Required		
49. Difficult To Promote		
50. Lack of Market		
51. Crowded Field		
52. Commodities		
53. Combination Products		
54. Entrenched Competition		
55. Instant Anachronism		

Total Positive _____

Less: Total Negative _____

NET: _____

Signed _____   Date: _____

POSITIVE FACTORS AFFECTING THE MARKETABILITY OF YOUR INVENTION

1. **Cost**. Is your invention cheaper to build or use than current knowledge would indicate?

2. **Weight**. Is your invention lighter (or heavier) in weight than what is already known, and is such change in weight a benefit? For example, if you've invented a new automobile or airplane engine, a reduction in weight is a great benefit. But if you've invented a new ballast material, obviously an increase in weight (provided it does not come at too great a cost in money or bulk) is a benefit.

3. **Size**. Is your invention smaller or larger in size or capacity than what is already known, and is such change in size a benefit?

4. **Safety/Health Factors**. Is your invention safer or healthier to use than what is already known? Clearly there is a strong trend in government and industry to improve the safety and reduce the possible chances for injury or harm in most products and processes, and this trend has given birth to many new inventions. Often a greater increase in cost and weight can be tolerated if certain safety and health benefits accrue.

5. **Speed**. Is your invention able to do a job faster (or slower) than its previous counterpart, and is such change in speed a benefit?

6. **Ease of Use**. Is your invention easier (or harder) to use, or learn to use, than its previously known counterpart? An example of a product where an increase in difficulty of use would be a benefit is a combination lock.

7. **Ease of Production**. Is your invention easier or cheaper (or harder or more expensive) to manufacture than previously known counterparts? Or can it be mass-produced, whereas previously known counterparts had to be made by hand? An example where making a device more difficult to manufacture would be of benefit is a credit card, which would be more difficult to forge if it were harder to make.

8. **Durability**. Does your invention last longer (or wear out sooner) than previously known counterparts? While built-in obsolescence is nothing to be admired, the stark economic reality is that many products, such as disposable razors, have earned their manufacturers millions by lasting for a shorter time than previously known counterparts.

9. **Repairability**. Is it easier to repair than previously known counterparts?

10. **Novelty**. Is your invention at all different from all previously known counterparts? Merely making an invention different may not appear to be an advantage per se, but it is usually a great advantage: It provides an alternate method or device for doing the job in case the first method or device ever encounters difficulties, for example, from government regulation, or in case the first device or method infringes a patent that you want to avoid infringing.

11. **Convenience/Social Benefit**. Does your invention make living easier or more convenient? Many inventions with a new function provide this advantage. Although you may question the ultimate wisdom and value of such gadgets as the electric knife, the remote-control TV, and the digital-readout clock, the reality remains that, in our relatively affluent society, millions of dollars have and are being made from devices that save labor and time (even though the time required to earn the after-tax money to buy the gadget is often greater than the time saved by using it). Then too, many new industries have been started by making an existing invention easier and convenient to use. Henry Ford didn't invent the automobile; he just produced it in volume and made it convenient for the masses to use. Ditto for George Eastman with his camera. And in modern times, the two Steves (Jobs and Wozniak) did much the same for the computer.

12. **Reliability**. Is your invention apt to fail less or need repair less often than previously known devices?

13. **Ecology**. Does your invention either make use of what previously were thought to be waste products? Does it reduce the use of limited natural resources? Does it produce less waste products, such as smoke, waste water, etc.? If so, you have an advantage which is very important and which should be emphasized strongly.

14. **Salability**. Is your invention easier to sell or market than existing counterparts?

15. **Appearance**. Does your invention provide a better-appearing design than existing counterparts?

16. **Viewability**. If your invention relates to eye use, does it present a brighter, clearer, or more viewable image? For example, a color TV with a brighter picture, or photochromic eyeglasses which automatically darken in sunlight are valuable inventions.

17. **Precision**. Does your invention operate or provide greater precision or more accuracy than existing counterparts?

18. **Noise**. Does your invention operate more quietly? Does it turn unpleasant noise into a more acceptable sound?

19. **Odor**. Does your invention emanate less or more unpleasant fumes or odors?

20. **Taste**. If your invention is edible or comes into contact with the taste buds (for example, a pill or a pipe stem), does it taste better? A foul taste (or smell) can also be an advantage, e.g., for poisons to prevent ingestion by children, and for telephone cables to deter chewing by rodents.

21. **Market Size**. Is there a larger market for your invention than for previously known devices? Because of climatic or legal restrictions, for example, certain inventions are only usable in small geographical areas. And because of economic factors, certain inventions may be limited to the relatively affluent. If your invention can obviate these restrictions, your potential market may be greatly increased, and this can be a significant advantage.

22. **Trend of Demand**. Is the trend of demand for your device increasing? Of course you should distinguish, if possible, between a trend and a fad. The first will provide a market for your invention while the second is likely to leave you high and dry unless you catch it in the beginning stages.

23. **Seasonal Demand**. Is your invention useful no matter what the season of the year? If so, it will have greater demand than a seasonal invention such as a sailboat.

24. **Difficulty of Market Penetration**. Is your device an improvement of a previously accepted device? If so, it will have an easier time penetrating the market than a device which provides a completely new function.

25. **Potential Competition**. Is your invention so simple, popular, or easy to manufacture that many imitators and copiers are likely to attempt to design around it, or break your patent as soon as it is brought out? Or is it a relatively complex, less popular, hard-to-manufacture device, which others would not be likely to produce in competition with you because of the large capital outlay required for tooling and production, etc?

26. **Quality**. Does your invention produce or provide a higher quality output or result than existing counterparts? For example, laser disks provide a much better audio quality than do phonorecords or magnetic tape.

27. **Excitement**. (The Neophile and the Conspicuous Consumer/Status Seeker). Almost all humans need some form of excitement in their lives: some obtain it by watching or participating in sports, others by the purchase of a new car or travel, and still others by the purchase of new products, such as a 50-inch TV, a laser disk player, or a friendly household robot. Such purchasers can be called "neophiles" (lovers of the new); their excitement comes from having and showing off their new "toy." Purchasers of expensive products, like the Mercedes Benz or a Rolex watch, commonly engage in what Thorsten Veblen has called "conspicuous consumption," and what we now call "status seeking." They enjoy showing off an expensive or unique item which they've acquired. Thus, if your invention can provide consumer excitement, either through sheer newness or through evidence of a costly purchase, it has a decided advantage.

28. **Mark-Up**. If your invention is in an excitement category (i.e., if it is very different, novel, innovative or luxurious), it can command a very high mark-up, a distinct selling advantage.

29. **Inferior Performance**. Yes, I'm serious! If your invention performs worse than comparable things which are already available, this can be a great advantage, if put to the proper use. Consider the 3M Company's fabulously successful Scotch® Post-It® note pads: Their novelty is simply that they have a strip of stickum which is inferior to known adhesives, thus providing removable self-stick notes. Here the invention may not be so much the discovery of an inferior adhesive as the discovery of a new use for it.

30. **"Sexy" Packaging**. If your invention is or comes in a "sexy" package, or is adaptable to being sold in such a package, this can be a great advantage. Consider the Haines l'Eggs® stockings where the package (shaped like an egg) made the product!

31. **Miscellaneous/Obviation of Specific Disadvantages of Existing Devices**. This is a catchall to cover anything I may have missed in the previous categories. Often the specific disadvantages which your invention overcomes will be quite obvious; they should be included here, nonetheless.

32. **Long Life Cycle**. If your invention has a generally long life cycle, i.e., it can be made and sold for many years before it becomes obsolete, this is an obvious strong advantage which will justify a capital expenditure for tooling, a big ad campaign, etc.

33. **Related Product Addability**. If your invention will usher in a new product line, as did the computer, where many related products such as disk drives and printers can be added, this will be an important advantage with potentially enhanced profits.

34. **Satisfies Existing Need**. If your invention will satisfy an existing, recognized need, such as preventing drug abuse, or avoiding auto collisions, your marketing difficulties will be greatly reduced.

NEGATIVE FACTORS LIKELY TO AFFECT THE MARKETABILITY OF YOUR INVENTION

Alas, every invention, no matter how great and disadvantage-free it seems, has one or more negative factors, even if the negative factor is merely the need to change, or design and produce, new production equipment. We've seen inventions and developments which were better in every way than what already existed, but which were not used solely because the improvement did not justify the cost of replacing existing production equipment, or the cost associated with manufacturing and promoting the device.

The negative factors of your invention are generally more important and require more consideration than the positive factors, since if your invention fails, it will obviously be one or more of the negative factors that cause it. Since all the positive factors listed above can be disadvantages when viewed in reverse, they should be carefully considered, but will not be reproduced here. For example, consider Factor #23, Seasonal Demand. This will be a negative, rather than a positive factor if the invention is something like skis or a holiday decoration, which does have a seasonal demand, rather than an all-year-around one.

1-34—REVERSE OF POSITIVE FACTORS LISTED ABOVE

35. **Legality**. Does your invention fail to comply with, or will its use fail to comply with, existing laws, regulations, and product and manufacturing requirements? Or, are administrative approvals required? If your invention carries legal difficulties with it, its acceptance will be problematic no matter how great its positive advantages are. And if ecological or safety approvals are required (for example, for drugs and automobiles), this will be viewed as a distinct disadvantage by prospective buyers.

36. **Operability**. Is it likely to work, or will significant additional design or technical development be required to make it practicable and workable?

37. **Development**. Is the product already designed for the market, or will additional engineering, material selection, appearance work, etc., be required?

38. **Profitability**. Because of possible requirements for exotic materials, difficult machining steps, great size, etc., is your invention likely to be difficult to sell at a profit?

39. **Obsolescence**. Is the field in which your invention is used likely to die out soon? If so, most manufacturers will not be willing to invest money in production facilities.

40. **Incompatibility**. Is your invention likely to be incompatible with existing patterns of use, customs, etc.?

41. **Product Liability Risk**. Is your invention in an area (such as drugs, firearms, contact sports, automobiles, etc.) where the risks of lawsuits against the manufacturer, due to product malfunction or injury from use, are likely to be greater than average?

42. Market Dependence. Is the sale of your invention dependent on a market for other goods, or is it useful in its own right? For example, an improved television tuner depends on the sale of televisions for its success, so that if the television market goes into a slump, the sales of your tuner certainly will fall also.

43. **Difficulty of Distribution**. Is your invention so large, fragile, perishable, etc., that it will be difficult or costly to distribute?

44. **Service Requirements**. Does your invention require frequent servicing and adjustment? If so, this is a distinct disadvantage. But consider the first commercial color TVs which, by any reasonable standard, were a service nightmare, but which made millions for their manufacturers.

45. **New Production Facilities Required**. Almost all inventions have this disadvantage. This is because the manufacture of anything new requires new tooling and production techniques.

46. **Inertia Must Be Overcome**. An example of a great invention that so far has failed because of user inertia is the Dvorak typewriter, which, although much faster and easier to use, was unable to overcome the awkward but entrenched Qwerty keyboard. If any invention is radically different, potential manufacturers, users and sellers will usually manifest some inertia, despite the invention's value.

47. **Too Advanced Technically**. In the 60s, a client received a very broad patent on a laser pumped by a chemical reaction explosion; we were very pleased with this patent. However it was so advanced at the time that the technology behind it is just now being implemented in connection with the "Star Wars" defense effort. Unfortunately, the patent expired in the meantime. The moral? Even if you have a great invention, make sure it can be commercially implemented within about 17 years.

48. **Substantial Learning Required**. If consumers will have to undergo substantial learning in order to use your invention, this is an obvious negative. An example: the early personal computers. On the other hand, some inventions, such as the automatically-talking clock, make a task even easier to do and thus have an obvious strong advantage.

49. **Difficult To Promote**. If it will be difficult to promote your invention, e.g., because it's technically complex, has subtle advantages, or is very expensive, large, awkward, etc., you've got an obvious disadvantage.

50. **Lack of Market**. If no market already exists for your invention, you'll have to convince the public that they need it—that is, that you have a "product in search of a market." While not a fatal flaw, and while this type of invention can be most profitable, you (or your licensee) will have to be prepared to expend substantial sums on promotion.

51. **Crowded Field**. If the field is already crowded, you'll have an uphill battle.

52. **Commodities**. If you've invented a new commodity—such as a better plastic, solvent, or grain—you'll face stiff price competition from the established, already streamlined standards.

53. **Combination Products**. If you've invented a "combination product"—that is, a product with two inventions that don't really groove together, like a stapler with a built-in beverage cup holder, people won't be

beating a path to your door. On the other hand, the clock-radio was just the ticket.

54. **Entrenched Competition.** Despite its overwhelming advantages, Edison had a terrible time promoting his light bulb because the gas companies fought him bitterly.

55. **Instant Anachronism.** A clever inventor in Oakland, California, invented a wonderful dictionary indexing device which made it much faster to look up any word. However, he was unable to sell it to any dictionary publisher because the dictionary is being replaced by computerized devices. His clever invention was an "instant anachronism."

Complete the Positive/Negative Factor's Evaluation form by assigning a weight to each listed factor, either in the positive or negative column. Also list and assign weights to any other factors you can think of which I've omitted. Then compute the sum of your positive and negative factors and determine the difference to come up with a rough idea of a net value for your invention. We suggest that you continue to pursue inventions with net values of 50 and up, that you direct your efforts elsewhere if your invention has a net value of less than 0, and that you make further critical evaluation of inventions with net values between 0 and 50.

Note: Again, we provide three tear-out copies of the Positive/Negative Factor's Evaluation form in Part G. The extra copies are in case you find others who can provide you with informed and impartial feedback on the commercial potential of your invention.

C2 POTENTIAL USER SURVEY

■ RECOMMENDED READING—*Patent It Yourself,* Chapter 4

As part of your marketing efforts you will want to show that your invention is likely to be well accepted. One way to do this is a survey among likely users. This involves showing the invention to several such users, collecting their comments, entering them in the notebook, and (if convenient) having the users sign and date their comments. A good way to conduct this survey is to exhibit at local inventors or new product fairs and showcases. Try a booth space in a local shopping mall. If your invention is patented, this type of survey can be done without having each person sign a Proprietary Materials Loan Agreement. The important thing is to get as much feedback from the potential customers as possible. A professional marketing firm would charge quite a bit to provide this same information. Use the tear-out form in Part G to make copies. Section C2 permits this systematic documentation for later disclosure to investors or manufacturers.

Note: The users should also sign a Proprietary Materials Loan Agreement if you are maintaining your invention as a trade secret (at least until a patent issues). Tear-out copies of this agreement are contained in Part G.

Potential User Survey

NAME AND DATE   AGREEMENT SIGNED?

1. _____

Comments: _____

_____

_____

_____

_____

_____

_____

_____

_____

_____

_____

_____

_____

_____

_____

Signed:_____   Date:_____

NAME AND DATE   AGREEMENT SIGNED?

2. _____

Comments: _____

_____

_____

_____

_____

_____

_____

_____

_____

_____

_____

_____

_____

_____

_____

Signed:_____   Date:_____

NAME AND DATE   AGREEMENT SIGNED?

3. _____

Comments: _____

_____

_____

_____

_____

_____

_____

_____

_____

_____

_____

_____

_____

_____

_____

_____

Signed:_____   Date:_____

NAME AND DATE   AGREEMENT SIGNED?

4. _____

Comments: _____

_____

_____

_____

_____

_____

_____

_____

_____

_____

_____

_____

_____

_____

_____

Signed:_____   Date:_____

NAME AND DATE   AGREEMENT SIGNED?

5. _____

Comments: _____

_____
_____
_____
_____
_____
_____
_____
_____
_____
_____
_____
_____
_____
_____
_____
_____

Signed:_____   Date:_____

NAME AND DATE   AGREEMENT SIGNED?

6. _____

Comments: _____

_____
_____
_____
_____
_____
_____
_____
_____
_____
_____
_____
_____
_____
_____
_____

Signed:_____   Date:_____

NAME AND DATE   AGREEMENT SIGNED?

7. _____

Comments: _____

_____

_____

_____

_____

_____

_____

_____

_____

_____

_____

_____

_____

_____

_____

Signed:_____   Date:_____

NAME AND DATE   AGREEMENT SIGNED?

8. _____

Comments: _____

_____

_____

_____

_____

_____

_____

_____

_____

_____

_____

_____

_____

_____

_____

Signed:_____   Date:_____

Potential User Survey

NAME AND DATE   AGREEMENT SIGNED?

9. _____

Comments: _____

_____

_____

_____

_____

_____

_____

_____

_____

_____

_____

_____

_____

_____

_____

_____

_____

Signed:_____   Date:_____

NAME AND DATE   AGREEMENT SIGNED?

10. _____

Comments: _____

_____

_____

_____

_____

_____

_____

_____

_____

_____

_____

_____

_____

_____

_____

_____

Signed:_____   Date:_____

C3 RELEVANT MARKET TRENDS

■ RECOMMENDED READING—*Do It Yourself Market Research* by A. B. Blankenship (McGraw-Hill), and *Low Cost Market Research* by Keith Gorton (Wiley)

To properly assess your invention's commercial potential, it's wise to carefully consider what existing trends, if any, will affect its acceptance in the marketplace. For instance, if you are inventing a new head cleaning device for 8-track tape players, you should consider that the trend toward cassettes is virtually eliminating the 8-track market. Obviously, with some inventions, such as head cleaning devices for 8-track tape players, you have little choice but to swim against the commercial stream, unless of course you decide that the current is so swift that you're better off putting the invention aside in favor of something else.

The forms we have designed for this part (C3) should help you to document (at least preliminarily) the trends which bear on the marketability of your invention. This documentation can be particularly essential if you plan to seek venture capital or a business partner. It also, of course, is the basis of any intelligent marketing strategy. When a potential investor or partner says, "tell me exactly how this thing will make money," the more persuasive your analysis of market trends, the better your chance of successfully completing the transaction.

Putting aside the head cleaning device for 8-track tape players as impracticable, given current market trends, let's say you go back to work and invent a new type of translucent bowling ball which contains holographic images that change as the ball rolls. The images could be attractive patterns, pictures of film or music celebrities, etc. If you want to sell this idea to a large manufacturer of related products, such as AMF or Brunswick, there is probably no point for you to spend time and money on an extensive market survey; they already know more about this area than you could ever hope to. If, on the other hand, you are seeking capital from someone who is not an expert in the field, you are going to have to convince him that the combination of bowling balls and holographic images is likely to be a hot item, at least in some areas of the country or among certain age groups. Simply put, will your bowling ball "play in Peoria"?

To answer this question for your invention, you will want to find data that tells you about:

• previous and forecasted buying patterns for related or competing products in your targeted marketing areas; and

• the projected size and buying power of the population groups of your most likely customers.

Where do you find this type of information? There are several specialized reference sources, available in large public libraries, which will provide you with enough information to at least partially answer these types of questions. Chief among these reference sources are:

• **Predicasts Forecasts.** This service abstracts information in newspapers, business magazines, trade journals and government reports that deals with market data, financial data, capacities, production, product development, trade, technology and forecasts. It is published quarterly by Predicasts.

• **U.S. Industrial Outlook.** This service contains the prospects for over 350 manufacturing and service industries. It is published by the U.S. Department of Commerce.

• **Statistical Reference Index.** This publication indexes and abstracts American statistical publications from private organizations and government sources. It is published by the Congressional Information Service (CIS) and is especially useful for obtaining key demographic information.

• **American Statistical Index.** This service Indexes and abstracts statistical information published by the U.S. Government. It is also useful for amassing demographic information.

• **Standard and Poor's Index.** This publication is published by Standard and Poor's Corporation and is useful for obtaining marketing information as it relates to companies.

• **Hine's Directory of Published Market Research.** This publication is a valuable directory to market research which has been carried out for other products and services.

Each of these publications contains detailed instructions on how to use it; reference librarians can also be quite helpful.

Of course, libraries are not the only place you can find commercial data. Vast amounts of information are stored in commercial computer databases and made available to you by "on-line" data services such as Dialog, InfoMaster (Western Union), IQUEST (Compuserve), and BRS. All you need to access this information is a personal computer, a modem, and money (lots of it). While the cost of using one of these on-line services (approximately $100 per hour) may sometimes be justified by your increased efficiency in searching mountains of facts and figures, efficiency tends to only come with a lot of practice. As this is an extremely expensive way to learn, the one-time user will seldom if ever benefit from using a computer as opposed to using the free resources available at any large public library.

A third alternative is to have someone else search the computer databases for you. Information searching has become a large and growing industry. One company, *Information on Demand*, located in Berkeley, California, will provide you the basic marketing information we suggest here at an average cost of between $300 and $500. They have an 800 number (800-227-0750) and can usually turn your request around in several days. While $500 may seem like a lot of money, it's our experience that the one-time user will probably pay more and get less if she conducts the computer search herself. Certainly, if the result greatly enhances your ability to convince others to produce or invest in your invention it will seem inexpensive in the long run. If you wish to find an information service closer to home, we suggest you look under "library," "reference" or "information" in your yellow pages index.[1]

Caution: Before you spend a lot of money for a search conducted by others, ask for and check references. The sources you use should not only be reputable but should be independently verifiable by anyone from whom you are seeking funds.

HOW TO USE FORM C3 TO RECORD DATA FROM THESE TYPES OF SOURCES

The Relevant Market Trends Form (C3) consists of three related sections:

• Regional Buying Patterns of Related Products, pages 1-3

• Predictions for Targeted Buying Groups, pages 4-6

• Conclusions, pages 7-9

---

[1] Public libraries are increasingly becoming connected with the computer databases described above and you may find it possible to obtain your information through the reference services offered by your local library at a fraction of what it would cost you to do your own computer search or obtain it from others.

There are three copies of each section to provide adequate room for more extensive surveys, or for the possibility of subsequent surveys for improved versions of your invention.

On the first three pages you should enter information you have located for sales of related products by geographical region. Taking our bowling ball example, related products could be (A) bowling balls, (B) holograms, (C) high tech recreation products (D) celebrity paraphernalia, and (E) bowling lanes. The relevant geographic regions would most likely begin with your local area and proceed to state or regional comparisons, national surveys, and even, if appropriate, international markets.

Regional Buying Patterns of Related Products

REGIONAL BUYING PATTERNS OF RELATED PRODUCTS				
	Product Name	Source of Information	Sales for Last Year Surveyed	Projected Sales
REGION:_____				
Product A	_____	_____	_____	_____
Product B	_____	_____	_____	_____
Product C	_____	_____	_____	_____
Product D	_____	_____	_____	_____
Product E	_____	_____	_____	_____

Pages 4-6, Predictions for Targeted Buying Groups, allow you to enter demographic information gleaned from your research. First, identify the potential purchaser groups that you think will account for the largest number of sales by Age, Sex, and Other. Then, for each group, look at their numbers as a percentage of the overall population in three promising market areas (regions). Also, take a look at the average disposable income of each group by region. For example, Group 1 (however you define it) may be those aged 13-18 of both sexes who bowl, while Group 2 may be identified in the "Other" category as owners of bowling alleys.

Predictions for Targeted Buying Groups

POTENTIAL PURCHASERS	AGE	SEX	OTHER	PREDICTED % OF SALES
Group 1				
Group 2				
Group 3				

	Source of Information	Last Year Surveyed	Projected
GROUP 1			
% of Population			
Region 1			
Region 2			
Region 3			
Disposable Income			
Region 1			
Region 2			
Region 3			

For Group 1, under "% of Pop." you would want to record both the present and predicted percentage of the entire population for this group in each region. This category would be irrelevant for Group 2 (who cares about how many bowling alley owners there are). Under "Disposable Income," you may want to record some data about the relative wealth of teenagers—this would bear on how much they have to spend on recreation. Your Group 2 data in this area might focus on such items as how much owners of bowling alleys spend annually replacing old balls and how much is spent on advertising to get more young people into bowling.

The last part of the form asks you to use the data entered in the first two parts to draw some conclusions about the market trends affecting your product. To see how this is done, let's again return to our example of the holographic bowling ball. You may have found that:

- the numbers of young people in the age groups you hope to sell your invention to are projected to decrease;

- the relative buying power of these young people is rapidly rising relative to the population as a whole;

- the sales of bowling balls and accessories are fairly steady;

- money spent on teen idol "essentials" and futuristic toys is steadily climbing; and

- young people bowl in much larger numbers in the Southeast than the Midwest.

While the first finding is essentially negative from a marketability standpoint, the other findings are essentially positive. Make a written record of both the positive and negative results of your survey and how they may influence your marketing strategy. In your presentation to a venture capital source, you should point out the increase in disposable income and interest in holograms and stars, and that you have decided to introduce your new sensation in the Southeast with the idea of creating a fad that will bring more young people into bowling alleys across the country. If you can back up this marketing approach with some solid information, you have a much better chance of being listened to.

REGIONAL BUYING PATTERNS OF RELATED PRODUCTS

	Product Name	Source of Information	Sales for Last Year Surveyed	Projected Sales

REGION:_____

Product A	_____	_____	_____	_____
Product B	_____	_____	_____	_____
Product C	_____	_____	_____	_____
Product D	_____	_____	_____	_____
Product E	_____	_____	_____	_____

REGION:_____

Product A	_____	_____	_____	_____
Product B	_____	_____	_____	_____
Product C	_____	_____	_____	_____
Product D	_____	_____	_____	_____
Product E	_____	_____	_____	_____

REGION:_____

Product A	_____	_____	_____	_____
Product B	_____	_____	_____	_____
Product C	_____	_____	_____	_____
Product D	_____	_____	_____	_____
Product E	_____	_____	_____	_____

REGIONAL BUYING PATTERNS OF RELATED PRODUCTS

	Product Name	Source of Information	Sales for Last Year Surveyed	Projected Sales
REGION:_____				
Product A	_____	_____	_____	_____
Product B	_____	_____	_____	_____
Product C	_____	_____	_____	_____
Product D	_____	_____	_____	_____
Product E	_____	_____	_____	_____
REGION:_____				
Product A	_____	_____	_____	_____
Product B	_____	_____	_____	_____
Product C	_____	_____	_____	_____
Product D	_____	_____	_____	_____
Product E	_____	_____	_____	_____
REGION:_____				
Product A	_____	_____	_____	_____
Product B	_____	_____	_____	_____
Product C	_____	_____	_____	_____
Product D	_____	_____	_____	_____
Product E	_____	_____	_____	_____

REGIONAL BUYING PATTERNS OF RELATED PRODUCTS

	Product Name	Source of Information	Sales for Last Year Surveyed	Projected Sales

REGION:_____

Product A	_____	_____	_____	_____
Product B	_____	_____	_____	_____
Product C	_____	_____	_____	_____
Product D	_____	_____	_____	_____
Product E	_____	_____	_____	_____

REGION:_____

Product A	_____	_____	_____	_____
Product B	_____	_____	_____	_____
Product C	_____	_____	_____	_____
Product D	_____	_____	_____	_____
Product E	_____	_____	_____	_____

REGION:_____

Product A	_____	_____	_____	_____
Product B	_____	_____	_____	_____
Product C	_____	_____	_____	_____
Product D	_____	_____	_____	_____
Product E	_____	_____	_____	_____

Predictions for Targeted Buying Groups

	POTENTIAL PURCHASERS	AGE	SEX	OTHER	PREDICTED % OF SALES
Group 1					
Group 2					
Group 3					

	Source of Information	Last Year Surveyed	Projected

GROUP 1

% of Population

Region 1 _____ _____ _____

Region 2 _____ _____ _____

Region 3 _____ _____ _____

Disposable Income

Region 1 _____ _____ _____

Region 2 _____ _____ _____

Region 3 _____ _____ _____

GROUP 2

% of Population

Region 1 _____ _____ _____

Region 2 _____ _____ _____

Region 3 _____ _____ _____

Disposable Income

Region 1 _____ _____ _____

Region 2 _____ _____ _____

Region 3 _____ _____ _____

GROUP 3

% of Population

Region 1 _____ _____ _____

Region 2 _____ _____ _____

Region 3 _____ _____ _____

Disposable Income

Region 1 _____ _____ _____

Region 2 _____ _____ _____

Region 3 _____ _____ _____

Relevant Market Trends

Predictions for Targeted Buying Groups

	POTENTIAL PURCHASERS	AGE	SEX	OTHER	PREDICTED % OF SALES
Group 1					
Group 2					
Group 3					

	Source of Information	Last Year Surveyed	Projected
GROUP 1			
% of Population			
Region 1			
Region 2			
Region 3			
Disposable Income			
Region 1			
Region 2			
Region 3			
GROUP 2			
% of Population			
Region 1			
Region 2			
Region 3			
Disposable Income			
Region 1			
Region 2			
Region 3			
GROUP 3			
% of Population			
Region 1			
Region 2			
Region 3			
Disposable Income			
Region 1			
Region 2			
Region 3			

Predictions for Targeted Buying Groups

POTENTIAL PURCHASERS	AGE	SEX	OTHER	PREDICTED % OF SALES
Group 1				
Group 2				
Group 3				

	Source of Information	Last Year Surveyed	Projected

GROUP 1

% of Population
  Region 1
  Region 2
  Region 3

Disposable Income
  Region 1
  Region 2
  Region 3

GROUP 2

% of Population
  Region 1
  Region 2
  Region 3

Disposable Income
  Region 1
  Region 2
  Region 3

GROUP 3

% of Population
  Region 1
  Region 2
  Region 3

Disposable Income
  Region 1
  Region 2
  Region 3

Conclusions

The demand for my product will likely increase because of these factors:_____

_____

_____

_____

_____

_____

_____

The demand could decrease because of these factors: _____

_____

_____

_____

_____

_____

To take advantage of the positive trends and overcome any projected negative developments, I propose to market my product in the following ways: _____

_____

_____

_____

_____

_____

_____

_____

Conclusions

The demand for my product will likely increase because of these factors:_____

_____

_____

_____

_____

_____

_____

The demand could decrease because of these factors: _____

_____

_____

_____

_____

_____

_____

To take advantage of the positive trends and overcome any projected negative developments, I propose to market my product in the following ways: _____

_____

_____

_____

_____

_____

_____

_____

Conclusions

The demand for my product will likely increase because of these factors:_____

_____

_____

_____

_____

_____

_____

The demand could decrease because of these factors: _____

_____

_____

_____

_____

_____

_____

To take advantage of the positive trends and overcome any projected negative developments, I propose to market my product in the following ways: _____

_____

_____

_____

_____

_____

_____

_____

C4 MANUFACTURER/DISTRIBUTOR EVALUATION

■ RECOMMENDED READING—*Patent It Yourself,* Chapter 11

The Inventor's Decision Chart asks you to decide whether you want to manufacture your invention yourself, and if so, whether you also plan to handle its distribution. The charts we provide here help you organize the facts on which thesedecisions should ultimately be based.

IF I WANT TO MANUFACTURE MYSELF

1. Items needed

   a. Facilities: _____

   _____

   b. Machinery/tools: _____

   _____

   c. Parts/inventory: _____

   _____

   d. New manufacturing processes: _____

   _____

   e. Employees: skill level and type: _____

   _____

   f. New technical skills: _____

   _____

   g. Government approval of site/process: _____

   _____

2. Forms needed: _____

   _____

3. Time needed to perfect the product: _____

   _____

4. Liability risks: _____

   _____

5. Volume I could produce: _____

   _____

6. Potential cost per unit and projected sale price: _____

   _____

7. How long to recover initial costs? _____

   _____

8. Profit from selling invention to an existing manufacturer: _____

   _____

Conclusions: _____

_____

_____

_____

_____

_____

IF I WANT TO DISTRIBUTE MYSELF

1. Items needed:

   a. Facilities: _____

   _____

   b. Inventory: _____

   _____

   c. Employees: _____

   _____

   d. New skills: _____

   _____

   e. Advertising: _____

   _____

2. Funds needed: _____

   _____

3. Distribution options: _____

   _____

4. Sales volume desired: _____

   _____

6. Time needed to achieve sales volume: _____

   _____

7. Liability risks: _____

   _____

8. Time needed to recover costs: _____

   _____

9. Percent/unit that would be paid to an existing distributor: _____

   _____

Conclusions: _____

_____

_____

_____

_____

_____

_____

_____

_____

_____

5   CHOOSING THE RIGHT COMPANY AND REACHING THE DECISION MAKER

If you decide to have someone else manufacture your invention, you need to decide which companies to approach. To do so efficiently:

• Choose companies that operate in your field, or in a related one.

• Consider size—depending on your product you may want to deal with a small entrepreneurial outfit, or a multinational.

• Consider location—companies with headquarters close to you are usually easier to approach.

• Consider company attitudes and products—do you like the company and its products?

• Consider marketing—if your product will require a good deal of consumer education to succeed (e.g., a machine that makes a cross between yogurt and peanut butter), will the company commit to a big advertising push or other long-term marketing technique that focuses on consumer education?

Companies can be researched in the same manner as products and services (see C3), either through the following written resources or in computer databases.

• *Thomas Register of American Manufacturers*

• *Dunn and Bradstreet's Million Dollar Directory*

• *Standard and Poor's Index*

• *MacRae's Verified Directory of Manufacturers' Representatives*

• *Encyclopedia of Associations* (which alerts you to the trade associations and journals that relate your invention)

• *Science Citation Index* (for scientific/technical information)

• *Business Periodical Index* (for business and finance information)

Information about any given company can also be obtained through a professional search company, as with the marketing information discussed in section C3 above.

You are most likely to do well with smaller companies near enoughto you so that you would have no difficulty making a visit to personally demonstrate the advantages of your invention. Choose a company that is in a similar product line and has the marketing, distribution, and advertising appropriate to sell your item. It is important to target companies that are doing well financially; even the simplest of ideas will require a substantial investment to bring to market.

The president of the company is who you must reach, if at all possible. He knows where he wants the company to go and he knows if the resources are available to get there. Try phoning before or after normal business hours—these guys are in the office ten and more hours a day, if you are lucky enough to catch them in town. Give a brief listing of the advantages of your product and ask if you can send them your Proprietary Materials Loan Agreement. If you have difficulty getting to the president, obtain an Annual Report and try contacting members of the Board of Directors or past, or retired presidents.

The universal key to making a good living as an inventor is perseverance, but it doesn't hurt to work smart. For instance, when seeking out an appropriate company for your invention, you might be wise to attend one or two trade shows. The contacts you can make at these types of gatherings can get more done for you than weeks in a library.

1st Choice

a. Name and Location:_____
    _____
    _____
    _____

b. Officers: _____
    _____
    _____
    _____

c. Current Products: _____
    _____
    _____

d. Sales Volume:_____
    _____

e. Advertising Budget:_____
    _____

f. Other:_____
    _____

2nd Choice

a. Name and Location:_____
    _____
    _____
    _____

b. Officers: _____
    _____
    _____
    _____

c. Current Products: _____
    _____
    _____

d. Sales Volume:_____
    _____

e. Advertising Budget:_____
    _____

f. Other:_____
    _____

3rd Choice

a. Name and Location:_____

_____

b. Officers: _____

_____

c. Current Products: _____

_____

d. Sales Volume:_____

e. Advertising Budget:_____

f. Other:_____

4th Choice

a. Name and Location:_____

_____

b. Officers: _____

_____

c. Current Products: _____

_____

d. Sales Volume:_____

e. Advertising Budget:_____

f. Other:_____

5th Choice

a. Name and Location:_____
   _____
   _____
   _____

b. Officers: _____
   _____
   _____
   _____

c. Current Products: _____
   _____
   _____

d. Sales Volume:_____
   _____

e. Advertising Budget:_____
   _____

f. Other:_____
   _____

6th Choice

a. Name and Location:_____
   _____
   _____
   _____

b. Officers: _____
   _____
   _____
   _____

c. Current Products: _____
   _____
   _____

d. Sales Volume:_____
   _____

e. Advertising Budget:_____
   _____

f. Other:_____
   _____

PART D

Financing

Part D: Financing

This part of *The Inventor's Notebook* helps you organize your search for funds to build and test, manufacture and distribute your invention. Section D1 guides you in arriving at a several estimates of how much capital you are likely to need in the course of getting your invention out of your head and into the marketplace. Section D2 is a checklist for the steps you should take before trying to sell the invention or before seeking funding to market it yourself. Finally, Section D3 helps you to keep track of your funding and/or sales efforts.

D1 DETERMINATION OF FUNDS NEEDED

■ RECOMMENDED READING—*Pratt's Guide to Venture Capital Sources* by Stanley E. Pratt (Venture Economics Inc., (annual edition)

Some inventors have the luxury of being able to invent without worrying about who will pick up the tab. Most of us, however, must keep a close eye on our budgets. This part of *The Inventor's Notebook* allows you to record cost estimates of your activities before initiating the building, testing, production and marketing phases of your invention. The notebook contains headings which prompt you to categorize the expenses appropriate to your invention. This means that you may be using some parts of form D1 and not others. Because there is usually a range of possibilities for costs, we provide space for a high, low, and middle estimate. The documentation called for in this section will help you design an appropriate business plan for your invention to show to persons or organizations you are seeking capital from.

We include three copies of the budget form. If you modify your invention after making one budget, you can fill out a sheet for the new version.

Budget

PURPOSE	HIGH ESTIMATE	MIDDLE ESTIMATE	LOW ESTIMATE
1. Build working model			
Parts	_____	_____	_____
Labor	_____	_____	_____
Subtotal	_____	_____	_____
2. Testing			
Parts	_____	_____	_____
Labor	_____	_____	_____
Subtotal	_____	_____	_____
3. Obtain Legal Protection			
Labor	_____	_____	_____
Legal fees	_____	_____	_____
Subtotal	_____	_____	_____
4. Test Marketing			
Survey	_____	_____	_____
Number of units	_____	_____	_____
Advertising/publicity	_____	_____	_____
Subtotal	_____	_____	_____
5. Establish Production			
Facilities	_____	_____	_____
Materials	_____	_____	_____
Employees	_____	_____	_____
Subtotal	_____	_____	_____
6. Other	_____	_____	_____
7. Grand Total	_____	_____	_____

PURPOSE	HIGH ESTIMATE	MIDDLE ESTIMATE	LOW ESTIMATE
1. Build working model			
Parts	_____	_____	_____
Labor	_____	_____	_____
Subtotal	_____	_____	_____
2. Testing			
Parts	_____	_____	_____
Labor	_____	_____	_____
Subtotal	_____	_____	_____
3. Obtain Legal Protection			
Labor	_____	_____	_____
Legal fees	_____	_____	_____
Subtotal	_____	_____	_____
4. Test Marketing			
Survey	_____	_____	_____
Number of units	_____	_____	_____
Advertising/publicity	_____	_____	_____
Subtotal	_____	_____	_____
5. Establish Production			
Facilities	_____	_____	_____
Materials	_____	_____	_____
Employees	_____	_____	_____
Subtotal	_____	_____	_____
6. Other	_____	_____	_____
7. Grand Total	_____	_____	_____

Budget

PURPOSE	HIGH ESTIMATE	MIDDLE ESTIMATE	LOW ESTIMATE
1. Build working model			
Parts	_____	_____	_____
Labor	_____	_____	_____
Subtotal	_____	_____	_____
2. Testing			
Parts	_____	_____	_____
Labor	_____	_____	_____
Subtotal	_____	_____	_____
3. Obtain Legal Protection			
Labor	_____	_____	_____
Legal fees	_____	_____	_____
Subtotal	_____	_____	_____
4. Test Marketing			
Survey	_____	_____	_____
Number of units	_____	_____	_____
Advertising/publicity	_____	_____	_____
Subtotal	_____	_____	_____
5. Establish Production			
Facilities	_____	_____	_____
Materials	_____	_____	_____
Employees	_____	_____	_____
Subtotal	_____	_____	_____
6. Other	_____	_____	_____
7. Grand Total	_____	_____	_____

D2 CHECKLIST FOR SELLING INVENTION/ SEEKING CAPITAL

■ RECOMMENDED READING—*Patent It Yourself,* Chapter 11

A number of important steps must be taken before you are ready to present your invention to the world. This part of the notebook provides space for you to keep track of these steps so that you can be equipped to make a thoroughly business-like presentation when you approach potential buyers. The first page is a checklist of steps necessary to prepare you for the presentation of your invention to potential purchasers or investors. The second page will help you focus on the essential points you want to cover, prepare responses to any possible questions, and reflect on the results of a practice presentation (we recommend that you practice your presentation with an associate or friend prior to the real thing). Your entries here should be brief notes to serve as reminders rather than full blown essays.

TWO ADDITIONAL SUGGESTIONS

One of the most sure-fire ways to raise money for a new idea is to get a significant number of purchase orders in hand. A good way to do this is to exhibit in one of the major trade shows in your product's industry. If you are going to do this you should have your homework done—samples that work and have a professional finish, the proper legal protection for your idea, sales literature, attractive packaging, an awareness of who the buyers are for the major accounts you want to land, and the ability to deliver on the orders, if need be with contract manufacturing. If this type of an event goes well, you will not only be able to obtain the financing you need, you may also receive offers from large companies to buy the rights to your invention.

Another way to substantiate the demand for your invention/product, and thereby increase the interest of investors, is from the responses generated by a press release in a national publication. Many magazines print news about new intentions or products. This does not cost you a thing other than the preparation of the materials you submit. Write to the individual publications for their guidelines on the preparations of press releases. Make sure that any photos you submit are of professional quality.

_____Made working model

_____Obtained legal protection

_____Test marketed

_____Prepared business plan

_____Return on investment projected

_____Recruited management team

           _____President or CEO

           _____Accounting

           _____Marketing

           _____Engineering

_____Surveyed manufacturers

_____Surveyed capital sources

_____Letter requesting appointment for presentation

           _____1st presentation

           _____2nd presentation

           _____3rd presentation

_____Phone call confirming appointment

           _____1st presentation

           _____2nd presentation

           _____3rd presentation

PERSONAL PRESENTATION NOTES

a. Advantages of my invention:_____
_____
_____
_____
_____

b. Anticipation of possible questions: _____
_____
_____
_____
_____

c. Profit potential:_____
_____
_____
_____
_____

d. Demonstration: _____
_____
_____
_____
_____

e. Trial presentation (rehearsal): _____
_____
_____
_____
_____

D3 FUNDING SOURCES AND RESULTS

■ RECOMMENDED READING—*Start Up Money,* Chapter 3

As you know, funding can come from many different sources (with their attendant pluses and minuses), and, it is likely to take more than one try to obtain the money you need. Make a record of those you contact and their response. If positive, how much money did they commit; if negative, why did they turn you down. This will give you a current assessment of how much more you need to ask for, and may prompt you to make changes in your method of presentation.

1. Relatives/Friends

    a. Name _____   Response_____

    _____

    b. Name _____   Response_____

    _____

    c. Name _____   Response_____

    _____

    d. Name _____   Response_____

    _____

    e. Name _____   Response_____

    _____

2. Banks

    a. Name _____   Response_____

    _____

    b. Name _____   Response_____

    _____

    c. Name _____   Response_____

    _____

    d. Name _____   Response_____

    _____

    e. Name _____   Response_____

    _____

3. Government Programs

    a. Name _____   Response_____

    _____

    b. Name _____   Response_____

    _____

    c. Name _____   Response_____

    _____

    d. Name _____   Response_____

    _____

    e. Name _____   Response_____

    _____

4. Venture Capital Companies

    a. Name _____   Response_____

    _____

    b. Name _____   Response_____

    _____

    c. Name _____   Response_____

    _____

    d. Name _____   Response_____

    _____

    e. Name _____   Response_____

    _____

PART E

Continuation Pages

Part E: Continuation Pages

This part contains 30 pages for use as continuation sheets for entries started on one of the forms in Parts A-D. The pages are blank except for the signing and witnessing statements at the bottom, and page numbers. When you use one of these pages, designate the page number on the form you are coming from. For instance if you are coming from Form A2 (Record the Building and Testing of Your Invention) and continuing your entry on page ___, you should enter "___" on Form A2 in the space provided.

For further description, see continuation page ___.

If there is no space for this information on the form you are coming from, simply write it in at the bottom.

Invented by:_____ Date: _____

Invented by:_____ Date: _____

Witnessed and understood by:_____ Date: _____

Witnessed and understood by:_____ Date: _____

Invented by:_____ Date: _____

Invented by:_____ Date: _____

Witnessed and understood by:_____ Date: _____

Witnessed and understood by:_____ Date: _____

Invented by:_____ Date:_____

Invented by:_____ Date:_____

Witnessed and understood by:_____ Date:_____

Witnessed and understood by:_____ Date:_____

Invented by:_____ Date: _____

Invented by:_____ Date: _____

Witnessed and understood by:_____ Date: _____

Witnessed and understood by:_____ Date: _____

Invented by:_____ Date:_____

Invented by:_____ Date:_____

Witnessed and understood by:_____ Date:_____

Witnessed and understood by:_____ Date:_____

Invented by:_____ Date: _____

Invented by:_____ Date: _____

Witnessed and understood by:_____ Date: _____

Witnessed and understood by:_____ Date: _____

Invented by:_____ Date: _____

Invented by:_____ Date: _____

Witnessed and understood by:_____ Date: _____

Witnessed and understood by:_____ Date: _____

Invented by:_____ Date: _____

Invented by:_____ Date: _____

Witnessed and understood by:_____ Date: _____

Witnessed and understood by:_____ Date: _____

Invented by:_____ Date:_____

Invented by:_____ Date:_____

Witnessed and understood by:_____ Date:_____

Witnessed and understood by:_____ Date:_____

Invented by:_____ Date: _____

Invented by:_____ Date: _____

Witnessed and understood by:_____ Date: _____

Witnessed and understood by:_____ Date: _____

Invented by:_____ Date: _____

Invented by:_____ Date: _____

Witnessed and understood by:_____ Date: _____

Witnessed and understood by:_____ Date: _____

Invented by:_____ Date: _____

Invented by:_____ Date: _____

Witnessed and understood by:_____ Date: _____

Witnessed and understood by:_____ Date: _____

Invented by:_____ Date: _____

Invented by:_____ Date: _____

Witnessed and understood by:_____ Date: _____

Witnessed and understood by:_____ Date: _____

Invented by:_____ Date: _____

Invented by:_____ Date: _____

Witnessed and understood by:_____ Date: _____

Witnessed and understood by:_____ Date: _____

Invented by:_____ Date: _____

Invented by:_____ Date: _____

Witnessed and understood by:_____ Date: _____

Witnessed and understood by:_____ Date: _____

Invented by:_____ Date: _____

Invented by:_____ Date: _____

Witnessed and understood by:_____ Date: _____

Witnessed and understood by:_____ Date: _____

Invented by:_____ Date: _____

Invented by:_____ Date: _____

Witnessed and understood by:_____ Date: _____

Witnessed and understood by:_____ Date: _____

Invented by:_____ Date:_____

Invented by:_____ Date:_____

Witnessed and understood by:_____ Date:_____

Witnessed and understood by:_____ Date:_____

Invented by:_____ Date: _____

Invented by:_____ Date: _____

Witnessed and understood by:_____ Date: _____

Witnessed and understood by:_____ Date: _____

Invented by:_____ Date: _____

Invented by:_____ Date: _____

Witnessed and understood by:_____ Date: _____

Witnessed and understood by:_____ Date: _____

Invented by:_____ Date: _____

Invented by:_____ Date: _____

Witnessed and understood by:_____ Date: _____

Witnessed and understood by:_____ Date: _____

Invented by:_____ Date: _____
Invented by:_____ Date: _____
Witnessed and understood by:_____ Date: _____
Witnessed and understood by:_____ Date: _____

Invented by:_____ Date:_____

Invented by:_____ Date:_____

Witnessed and understood by:_____ Date:_____

Witnessed and understood by:_____ Date:_____

Invented by:_____ Date: _____

Invented by:_____ Date: _____

Witnessed and understood by:_____ Date: _____

Witnessed and understood by:_____ Date: _____

Invented by:_____ Date: _____

Invented by:_____ Date: _____

Witnessed and understood by:_____ Date: _____

Witnessed and understood by:_____ Date: _____

Invented by:_____ Date: _____

Invented by:_____ Date: _____

Witnessed and understood by:_____ Date: _____

Witnessed and understood by:_____ Date: _____

P A R T F

Bibliography

Part F: Bibliography—Books of Use and Interest

Throughout this notebook we have suggested specific outside readings for each section. This part is designed to help you find additional print resources that can extend your understanding of issues addressed in this book and help you answer questions and address issues not covered by this book. We list these suggested resources under the following categories:

• Government publications;

• Patent law;

• Trade secret and trademark law;

• Business; and

• General interest

We also provide a brief comment where the title of the book or source isn't self-explanatory. Most books which can't be found in a general or business library may be found in a law library. In a few instances the resources are most likely only available in a Patent Depository Library. We indicate this fact with an asterisk following the entry. This bibliography is not exclusive by any means. If you browse in an appropriate library or bookstore you'll probably find many other valuable books of interest. Prices aren't indicated since they are subject to rapid change.

GOVERNMENT PUBLICATIONS

Annual Index of Patents. Issued yearly in two volumes: *Patentees* and *Titles of Inventions.* U.S. Government Printing Office (GPO), Washington, DC 20402. Comes out long after the end of year to which it pertains—for instance, in September for the previous year.*

Attorneys and Agents Registered to Practice before the U.S. Patent and Trademark Office. Annual. Government Printing Office. Contains alphabetical and geographical listings of all patent and trademark attorneys and patent agents.

Classification Definitions. Many looseleaf volumes. Contains definitions for each of 66,000 subclasses.*

Rules of Practice in Patent Cases. Government Printing Office. Revised annually. The PTO's Rules of Practice. A must for all who prosecute their own patent applications. Almost always incomplete due to frequent rule changes. Look in *Official Gazette* for later rules.

Guide for Patent Draftsmen. Government Printing Office

Index to Classification. Loose-leaf. Contains 66,000 subclasses and cross-references arranged alphabetically.

Manual of Classification. Loose-leaf. Contains 300 search classes for patents arranged numerically, together with subclasses in each class.

Manual of Patent Examining Procedure. Revisions issued several times per year. GPO. Called "the patent examiner's bible," the MPEP provides answers to most questions about patent prosecution.

LAW RESOURCES RELATING TO PATENTS

Corpus Juris Secundum, Vol. 69, Patents. A legal encyclopedia which will answer almost any question on patent law. West Pub. Co., St. Paul, 1958 (supplemented annually). Any law library.

Elias, *Patent, Copyright and Trademark: The Intellectual Property Law Dictionary.* Nolo, Berkeley.

Greer Jr., T.J. *Writing and Understanding U.S. Patent Claims; A Programmed Workbook.* Michie, 1979.

Journal of the Patent Office Society. Monthly. Box 2600, Arlington, VA 22202. Contains articles on patent law and advertisements by patent services (e.g., draftspersons, drawing reproducers, searchers).

Landis, J.L. *The Mechanics of Patent Claim Drafting,* 2d ed. Practicing Law Instititute, 810 Seventh Avenue, NY 10019, 1974.

Patent and Trademark Laws. BNA. Revised annually.

Patent Official Gazette. Issued each Tuesday. Government Printing Office. Contains drawing and main claim of every patent issued each week, miscellaneous notices, new PTO rules; lists inventors, assignees, etc.[*]

Questions and Answers about Plant Patents. A free pamphlet issued by the PTO.

Nordhaus, R.C. *Patent License Agreements.* Jural, Chicago, 1976.

Patent Law Assn. of Chicago. *Tax Guide for Patents, Trademarks, and Copyrights.* Clark Boardman, 1981.

Rosenberg, P.D. *Patent Law Fundamentals.* Clark Boardman, 1980. Updated annually.

White, R.S. *Patent Litigation Procedure & Tactics.* Matthew Bender, New York, 1974.

LAW RESOURCES RELATING TO TRADE SECRETS AND TRADEMARKS

McGrath & Elias, *Trademark: How To Name a Business & Product.* Nolo, Berkeley.

Questions and Answers about Trademarks. A free pamphlet issued by the PTO.

Trademark Official Gazette. Government Printing Office. Lists trademarks published for opposition and registered each week.

Milgrim, R.M., *Trade Secrets.* Matthew Bender, New York, 1967, updated annually.

RESOURCES RELATING TO BUSINESS

Adams, A.B. *Apollo Handbook of Practical Public Relations.* Apollo Editions, New York, 1970. How to get publicity.

Applied Sciences and Technology Index. H.W. Wilson Co. Bronx, NY 10452. Lists engineering, scientific, and industrial periodicals by subject.

Ayer Directory of Newspapers and Periodicals. Annual. Ayer Press, Philadelphia. Lists United States newspapers and magazines geographically.

Bacon's Publicity Checker—Magazines, Bacon's Publicity Checker— Newspapers. Annual. Bacon Pub. Co., Chicago. Classifies all sources of publicity.

Bragonier Jr., R. and Fisher, J. *What's What; A Visual Glossary of Everyday Objects.* Ballantine, 1981.

Brown, D. *The Entrepreneur's Manual.* Ballantine, 1981.

California Manufacturers Register. Annual. 1115 S. Boyle Ave., Los Angeles, CA 90023.

Conover Mast Purchasing Directory. Conover Mast, Denver. Annual. Three volumes. Manufacturers listed alphabetically and by products. Also lists trademarks.

Dible, D.M. *Up Your Own Organization.* Entrepreneur Press, c/o Hawthorn Books, New York. How to start and finance a business.

Drucker, P. *Innovation and Entrepreneurship,* Harper & Row, 1985. How any organization can become entrepreneurial.

Dun & Bradstreet Reference Book. Six issues per year. Lists three million businesses in the United States and Canada. D&B also publishes specialized reference books and directories, e.g., *Apparel Trades Book* and *Metalworking Marketing Directory.*

Fisher, R. & Ury, W. *Getting to Yes; Negotiating Agreements Without Giving In.* Penguin, 1981.

Guide to American Directories. 9th ed. B. Klein Pubs., New York, 1975. Lists directories by industry, profession, and function.

International Yellow Pages. R.H. Donnelley Corp., New York. Similar to local Yellow Pages, but provides foreign business listings.

Lynn, G. S., *From Concept to Market.* John Wiley and Sons, 1987.

MacRae's Blue Book. MacRae's Blue Book Co., Hinsdale, IL. Sources of industrial equipment, products, and materials. Also lists trademarks.

Paige, R.E. *Complete Guide to Making Money with Your Ideas and Inventions.* Barnes & Noble, New York, 1976. Guide to invention marketing.

Petillon, L.R. & Hull, R.J. *R & D Partnerships.* Clark Boardman, 1985.

Pratt, S.E., ed. *How to Raise Venture Capital.* Scribners, New York, 1982.

Rich, S.R. & Gumpert, D. *Business Plans That Win Money: Lessons From the MIT Enterprises Forum.* Harper & Row, 1985.

Small Business Administration. The SBA's list of free publications has three sections: "Management Aids," "Small Marketer's Aids," and "Small Business Bibiliographies." Listed are dozens of excellent, concise business pamphlets, such as no. 82, *Reducing the Risks in Product Development,* and 6.004, *Selecting the Legal Structure for Your Firm.* Order from your local SBA office or SBA, Washington DC 20416.

Thomas Register of American Manufacturers. Thomas Pub., New York. Eleven volumes. Similar to *Conover Mast Directory* above.

Tolly, S. *Advertising and Marketing Research.* Nelson-Hall, Chicago, 1977.

Ulrich's International Periodicals Directory. R.R. Bowker Co., New York. Lists periodicals by subject.

Venture Capital Monthly. S.M. Rubel Co., Chicago,.

RESOURCES OF GENERAL INTEREST TO INVENTORS

The Story of the U.S. PTO. Government Printing Office. 1985.

Clark, R.W. *Edison—The Man Who Made the Future.* Putnam, New York, 1977. Provides a good overview of how to get creative ideas to market.

Florman, S.C. *The Existential Pleasures of Engineering.* St. Martens, 1976. A brilliant, eloquent panegyric of technology; a crushing blow to Reich, Mumford, Rozak, et al.

Harness, Charles R., Esq. *The Catalyst.* Pocket Books, New York, 1980. Science fiction story involving a patent attorney, an invention, and an interference. Helps the inventor understand the need for accurate documentation of inventive efforts.

Inventing: How the Masters Did It. Moore Pub., Durham, NC, 1974.

Lessing, L. *Man of High Fidelity: Edwin Howard Armstrong.* Lippincott, Philadelphia, 1956. Biography of the inventor of frequency modulation; he committed suicide because of the delays and difficulties of patent litigation against the large radio companies, but his widow eventually collected millions in settlements.

Martindale-Hubbell Law Directory. Martindale-Hubbell, New York. Annual. Lists patent attorneys by geographical area (including some foreign) and give ages, colleges, and sometimes other information about attorneys. Any law library.

The National Inventors Hall of Fame. *Biographies of Inductees.* NIHF Foundation, Room 1D01, Crystal Plaza 3, 2001 Jeff Davis Hwy., Arlington, VA 22202. Free.

Ord-Hume, A., *Perpetual Motion: The History of An Obsession.* St. Martens, 1981. A must if you're filing on a "perpetual motion" machine.

Walsh, J.E. *One Day at Kitty Hawk.* Crowell, New York, 1975. The story of the development and sale of rights to the airplane.

PART G

Forms

Part G: Forms

■ RECOMMENDED READING—*Patent It Yourself,* Chapters 1 and 3

In this part we provide you with:

• 1 tear-out copy of the Potential User Survey Form

• 5 tear-out copies of the Consultants Work Agreement

• 5 copies of a "Proprietary Materials Agreement" and

• 5 copies of the "Positive/Negative Factors Evaluation" form discussed in C1.

The Proprietary Materials Loan Agreement is designed for use when you disclose significant details about an unpatented invention to potential developers, investors, evaluators, or partners. The form binds the recipient of the information to confidentiality so you can preserve your invention as a trade secret up until the time you are granted a patent (or beyond, in the event your patent application is denied).

Although the form speaks in terms of a loan of materials, it is also appropriate when information is disclosed orally or in writing, or when the invention is displayed or demonstrated. Simply fill out the blanks and have the person to whom you are disclosing information sign the form before the disclosure. Then:

• put the form with your other papers related to your invention; and

• enter the person's name in Section B6 of the notebook (Contacts with Others), along with a notation that the agreement has been signed.

If a person signing one of these forms later discloses information about your invention to others, you may be able to obtain court relief (assuming you have taken the other steps necessary to preserve your invention as a trade secret).

The five copies of our Positive/Negative Factors Evaluation form are for use in the event you involve friends, family or associates in the process discussed in C1.

Potential User Survey

NAME AND DATE   AGREEMENT SIGNED?

1 _____

Comments: _____

_____

_____

_____

_____

_____

_____

_____

_____

_____

_____

_____

_____

_____

_____

_____

Signed:_____   Date:_____

NAME AND DATE   AGREEMENT SIGNED?

2. _____

Comments: _____

_____

_____

_____

_____

_____

_____

_____

_____

_____

_____

_____

_____

_____

_____

Signed:_____   Date:_____

Consultant's Work Agreement

1. **Parties:** This Work Agreement is made between the following parties:

   Name(s) _____

   Address(es): _____

   _____

   (hereinafter Contractor), and

   Name(s): _____

   Address(es): _____

   _____

   (hereinafter Consultant).

2. **Name of Project:** _____

   _____

   _____

3. **Work To Be Performed By Consultant:** _____

   _____

   _____

4. **Work/Payment Schedule:** _____

   _____

   _____

5. **Date:** This Agreement shall be effective as of the latter date below written.

6. **Recitals:** Contractor has one or more ideas relating to the above project and desires to have such project developed more completely, as specified in the above statement of Work. Consultant has certain skills desired by Contractor relating to performance of the above Work.

7. **Performance:** Consultant will perform the above work for Contractor, in accordance with the above-scheduled Work/Payment Schedule and Contractor will make the above scheduled payments to Consultant. Any changes to the Work To Be Performed or the Work/Payment Schedule shall be described in a writing referring to this Agreement and signed and dated by both parties. Time is of the essence of this Agreement, and if Consultant fails to perform according to the above work schedule, contractor may (a) void this agreement and pay consultant 50% of what would otherwise be due, or (b) require that Consultant pay contractor a penalty of $_____ per day.

8. **Intellectual Property:** All intellectual property, including trademarks, writings, information, trade secrets, inventions, discoveries, or improvements, whether or not registerable or patentable, which are conceived, constructed, or written by Consultant and arise out of or are related to work and services performed under this agreement, are, or shall become and remain the sole and exclusive property of Contractor, whether or not such intellectual property is conceived during the time such work and services are performed or billed.

9A. **Protection Of Intellectual Property:** Contractor and Consultant recognize that under US patent laws, all patent applications must be filed in the name of the true and actual inventor(s) of the subject matter sought to be patented. Thus if Consultant makes any patentable inventions relating to the above project, Consultant agrees to be named as an applicant in any US patent application(s) filed on such invention(s). Actual ownership of such patent applications shall be governed by clause 8.

9B. Consultant shall promptly disclose to Contractor in writing all information pertaining to any intellectual property generated or conceived by Consultant under this Agreement. Consultant hereby assigns and agrees to assign all of Consultant's rights to such intellectual property, including patent rights and foreign priority rights. Consultant hereby expressly agrees, without further charge for time, to do all things and sign all documents deemed by Contractor to be necessary or appropriate to invest in intellectual property, including obtaining for and vesting in Contractor all U.S. and foreign patents and patent applications which Contractor desires to obtain to cover such intellectual property, provided that Contractor shall bear all expenses relating thereto. All reasonable local travel time and expenses shall be borne by Consultant.

10. **Trade Secrets:** Consultant recognizes that all information relating to the above Project disclosed to Consultant by Contractor, and all information generated by Consultant in the performance of the above Work, is a valuable trade secret of Contractor and Consultant shall treat all such information as strictly confidential, during and after the performance of Work under this Agreement. Specifically Consultant shall not reveal, publish, or communicate any such information to anyone other than Contractor, and shall safeguard all such information from access to anyone other than Contractor, except upon the express written authorization of Contractor. This clause shall not apply to any information which Consultant can document in writing is presently in or enters the public domain from a bona fide source other than Consultant.

11. **Return Of Property:** Consultant agree to return all written materials and objects received from Contractor, to deliver to Contractor all objects and a copy (and all copies and originals if requested by Contractor) of all written materials resulting from or relating to work performed under this Agreement, and not to deliver to any person, organization, or publisher, or cause to be published, any such written material without prior written authorization.

12. **Conflicts Of Interest:** Consultant recognizes a fiduciary obligation to Contractor arising out of the work and services performed under this agreement and accordingly will not offer Consultant's service to or perform services for any competitor, potential or actual, of Contractor for the above Project, or perform any other acts which may result in any conflict of interest by Consultant, during and after the term of this Agreement.

13. **Mediation And Arbitration:** If any dispute arises under this Agreement, the parties shall negotiate in good faith to settle such dispute. If the parties cannot resolve such dispute themselves, then either party may submit the dispute to mediation by a mediator approved by both parties. If the parties cannot agree to any mediator, or if either party does not wish to abide by any decision of the mediator, they shall submit the dispute to arbitration by any mutually-acceptable arbitrator, or the American Arbitration Association (AAA). If the AAA is selected, the arbitration shall take place under the auspices of the nearest branch of such to both parties. The costs of the arbitration proceeding shall be borne according to the decision of the arbitrator, who may apportion costs equally, or in accordance with any finding or fault or lack of good faith of either party. The arbitrator's award shall be non-appealable and enforceable in any court of competent jurisdiction.

14. **Governing Law:** This Agreement shall be governed by and interpreted under and according to the laws of the State of _____ .

15. **Signatures:** The parties have indicated their agreement to all of the above terms by signing this Agreement on the respective dates below indicated. Each party has received an original signed copy hereof.

Contractor:

Date: _____

_____

Consultant:

Date: _____

_____

Consultant's Work Agreement

1. **Parties:** This Work Agreement is made between the following parties:

   Name(s) _____

   Address(es): _____

   _____

   (hereinafter Contractor), and

   Name(s): _____

   Address(es): _____

   _____

   (hereinafter Consultant).

2. **Name of Project:** _____

   _____

   _____

3. **Work To Be Performed By Consultant:** _____

   _____

   _____

4. **Work/Payment Schedule:** _____

   _____

   _____

5. **Date:** This Agreement shall be effective as of the latter date below written.

6. **Recitals:** Contractor has one or more ideas relating to the above project and desires to have such project developed more completely, as specified in the above statement of Work. Consultant has certain skills desired by Contractor relating to performance of the above Work.

7. **Performance:** Consultant will perform the above work for Contractor, in accordance with the above-scheduled Work/Payment Schedule and Contractor will make the above scheduled payments to Consultant. Any changes to the Work To Be Performed or the Work/Payment Schedule shall be described in a writing referring to this Agreement and signed and dated by both parties. Time is of the essence of this Agreement, and if Consultant fails to perform according to the above work schedule, contractor may (a) void this agreement and pay consultant 50% of what would otherwise be due, or (b) require that Consultant pay contractor a penalty of $_____ per day.

8. **Intellectual Property:** All intellectual property, including trademarks, writings, information, trade secrets, inventions, discoveries, or improvements, whether or not registerable or patentable, which are conceived, constructed, or written by Consultant and arise out of or are related to work and services performed under this agreement, are, or shall become and remain the sole and exclusive property of Contractor, whether or not such intellectual property is conceived during the time such work and services are performed or billed.

9A. **Protection Of Intellectual Property:** Contractor and Consultant recognize that under US patent laws, all patent applications must be filed in the name of the true and actual inventor(s) of the subject matter sought to be patented. Thus if Consultant makes any patentable inventions relating to the above project, Consultant agrees to be named as an applicant in any US patent application(s) filed on such invention(s). Actual ownership of such patent applications shall be governed by clause 8.

9B. Consultant shall promptly disclose to Contractor in writing all information pertaining to any intellectual property generated or conceived by Consultant under this Agreement. Consultant hereby assigns and agrees to assign all of Consultant's rights to such intellectual property, including patent rights and foreign priority rights. Consultant hereby expressly agrees, without further charge for time, to do all things and sign all documents deemed by Contractor to be necessary or appropriate to invest in intellectual property, including obtaining for and vesting in Contractor all U.S. and foreign patents and patent applications which Contractor desires to obtain to cover such intellectual property, provided that Contractor shall bear all expenses relating thereto. All reasonable local travel time and expenses shall be borne by Consultant.

10. **Trade Secrets:** Consultant recognizes that all information relating to the above Project disclosed to Consultant by Contractor, and all information generated by Consultant in the performance of the above Work, is a valuable trade secret of Contractor and Consultant shall treat all such information as strictly confidential, during and after the performance of Work under this Agreement. Specifically Consultant shall not reveal, publish, or communicate any such information to anyone other than Contractor, and shall safeguard all such information from access to anyone other than Contractor, except upon the express written authorization of Contractor. This clause shall not apply to any information which Consultant can document in writing is presently in or enters the public domain from a bona fide source other than Consultant.

11. **Return Of Property:** Consultant agree to return all written materials and objects received from Contractor, to deliver to Contractor all objects and a copy (and all copies and originals if requested by Contractor) of all written materials resulting from or relating to work performed under this Agreement, and not to deliver to any person, organization, or publisher, or cause to be published, any such written material without prior written authorization.

12. **Conflicts Of Interest:** Consultant recognizes a fiduciary obligation to Contractor arising out of the work and services performed under this agreement and accordingly will not offer Consultant's service to or perform services for any competitor, potential or actual, of Contractor for the above Project, or perform any other acts which may result in any conflict of interest by Consultant, during and after the term of this Agreement.

13. **Mediation And Arbitration:** If any dispute arises under this Agreement, the parties shall negotiate in good faith to settle such dispute. If the parties cannot resolve such dispute themselves, then either party may submit the dispute to mediation by a mediator approved by both parties. If the parties cannot agree to any mediator, or if either party does not wish to abide by any decision of the mediator, they shall submit the dispute to arbitration by any mutually-acceptable arbitrator, or the American Arbitration Association (AAA). If the AAA is selected, the arbitration shall take place under the auspices of the nearest branch of such to both parties. The costs of the arbitration proceeding shall be borne according to the decision of the arbitrator, who may apportion costs equally, or in accordance with any finding or fault or lack of good faith of either party. The arbitrator's award shall be non-appealable and enforceable in any court of competent jurisdiction.

14. **Governing Law:** This Agreement shall be governed by and interpreted under and according to the laws of the State of _____ .

15. **Signatures:** The parties have indicated their agreement to all of the above terms by signing this Agreement on the respective dates below indicated. Each party has received an original signed copy hereof.

Contractor:

Date: _____   _____

Consultant:

Date: _____   _____

Consultant's Work Agreement

1. **Parties:** This Work Agreement is made between the following parties:

   Name(s) _____

   Address(es): _____

   _____

   (hereinafter Contractor), and

   Name(s): _____

   Address(es): _____

   _____

   (hereinafter Consultant).

2. **Name of Project:** _____

   _____

   _____

3. **Work To Be Performed By Consultant:** _____

   _____

   _____

4. **Work/Payment Schedule:** _____

   _____

   _____

5. **Date:** This Agreement shall be effective as of the latter date below written.

6. **Recitals:** Contractor has one or more ideas relating to the above project and desires to have such project developed more completely, as specified in the above statement of Work. Consultant has certain skills desired by Contractor relating to performance of the above Work.

7. **Performance:** Consultant will perform the above work for Contractor, in accordance with the above-scheduled Work/Payment Schedule and Contractor will make the above scheduled payments to Consultant. Any changes to the Work To Be Performed or the Work/Payment Schedule shall be described in a writing referring to this Agreement and signed and dated by both parties. Time is of the essence of this Agreement, and if Consultant fails to perform according to the above work schedule, contractor may (a) void this agreement and pay consultant 50% of what would otherwise be due, or (b) require that Consultant pay contractor a penalty of $_____ per day.

8. **Intellectual Property:** All intellectual property, including trademarks, writings, information, trade secrets, inventions, discoveries, or improvements, whether or not registerable or patentable, which are conceived, constructed, or written by Consultant and arise out of or are related to work and services performed under this agreement, are, or shall become and remain the sole and exclusive property of Contractor, whether or not such intellectual property is conceived during the time such work and services are performed or billed.

9A. **Protection Of Intellectual Property:** Contractor and Consultant recognize that under US patent laws, all patent applications must be filed in the name of the true and actual inventor(s) of the subject matter sought to be patented. Thus if Consultant makes any patentable inventions relating to the above project, Consultant agrees to be named as an applicant in any US patent application(s) filed on such invention(s). Actual ownership of such patent applications shall be governed by clause 8.

9B. Consultant shall promptly disclose to Contractor in writing all information pertaining to any intellectual property generated or conceived by Consultant under this Agreement. Consultant hereby assigns and agrees to assign all of Consultant's rights to such intellectual property, including patent rights and foreign priority rights. Consultant hereby expressly agrees, without further charge for time, to do all things and sign all documents deemed by Contractor to be necessary or appropriate to invest in intellectual property, including obtaining for and vesting in Contractor all U.S. and foreign patents and patent applications which Contractor desires to obtain to cover such intellectual property, provided that Contractor shall bear all expenses relating thereto. All reasonable local travel time and expenses shall be borne by Consultant.

10. **Trade Secrets:** Consultant recognizes that all information relating to the above Project disclosed to Consultant by Contractor, and all information generated by Consultant in the performance of the above Work, is a valuable trade secret of Contractor and Consultant shall treat all such information as strictly confidential, during and after the performance of Work under this Agreement. Specifically Consultant shall not reveal, publish, or communicate any such information to anyone other than Contractor, and shall safeguard all such information from access to anyone other than Contractor, except upon the express written authorization of Contractor. This clause shall not apply to any information which Consultant can document in writing is presently in or enters the public domain from a bona fide source other than Consultant.

11. **Return Of Property:** Consultant agree to return all written materials and objects received from Contractor, to deliver to Contractor all objects and a copy (and all copies and originals if requested by Contractor) of all written materials resulting from or relating to work performed under this Agreement, and not to deliver to any person, organization, or publisher, or cause to be published, any such written material without prior written authorization.

12. **Conflicts Of Interest:** Consultant recognizes a fiduciary obligation to Contractor arising out of the work and services performed under this agreement and accordingly will not offer Consultant's service to or perform services for any competitor, potential or actual, of Contractor for the above Project, or perform any other acts which may result in any conflict of interest by Consultant, during and after the term of this Agreement.

13. **Mediation And Arbitration:** If any dispute arises under this Agreement, the parties shall negotiate in good faith to settle such dispute. If the parties cannot resolve such dispute themselves, then either party may submit the dispute to mediation by a mediator approved by both parties. If the parties cannot agree to any mediator, or if either party does not wish to abide by any decision of the mediator, they shall submit the dispute to arbitration by any mutually-acceptable arbitrator, or the American Arbitration Association (AAA). If the AAA is selected, the arbitration shall take place under the auspices of the nearest branch of such to both parties. The costs of the arbitration proceeding shall be borne according to the decision of the arbitrator, who may apportion costs equally, or in accordance with any finding or fault or lack of good faith of either party. The arbitrator's award shall be non-appealable and enforceable in any court of competent jurisdiction.

14. **Governing Law:** This Agreement shall be governed by and interpreted under and according to the laws of the State of _____ .

15. **Signatures:** The parties have indicated their agreement to all of the above terms by signing this Agreement on the respective dates below indicated. Each party has received an original signed copy hereof.

Contractor:

Date: _____   _____

Consultant:

Date: _____   _____

Consultant's Work Agreement

1. **Parties:** This Work Agreement is made between the following parties:

   Name(s) _____

   Address(es): _____

   _____

   (hereinafter Contractor), and

   Name(s): _____

   Address(es): _____

   _____

   (hereinafter Consultant).

2. **Name of Project:** _____

   _____

   _____

3. **Work To Be Performed By Consultant:** _____

   _____

   _____

4. **Work/Payment Schedule:** _____

   _____

   _____

5. **Date:** This Agreement shall be effective as of the latter date below written.

6. **Recitals:** Contractor has one or more ideas relating to the above project and desires to have such project developed more completely, as specified in the above statement of Work. Consultant has certain skills desired by Contractor relating to performance of the above Work.

7. **Performance:** Consultant will perform the above work for Contractor, in accordance with the above-scheduled Work/Payment Schedule and Contractor will make the above scheduled payments to Consultant. Any changes to the Work To Be Performed or the Work/Payment Schedule shall be described in a writing referring to this Agreement and signed and dated by both parties. Time is of the essence of this Agreement, and if Consultant fails to perform according to the above work schedule, contractor may (a) void this agreement and pay consultant 50% of what would otherwise be due, or (b) require that Consultant pay contractor a penalty of $_____ per day.

8. **Intellectual Property:** All intellectual property, including trademarks, writings, information, trade secrets, inventions, discoveries, or improvements, whether or not registerable or patentable, which are conceived, constructed, or written by Consultant and arise out of or are related to work and services performed under this agreement, are, or shall become and remain the sole and exclusive property of Contractor, whether or not such intellectual property is conceived during the time such work and services are performed or billed.

9A. **Protection Of Intellectual Property:** Contractor and Consultant recognize that under US patent laws, all patent applications must be filed in the name of the true and actual inventor(s) of the subject matter sought to be patented. Thus if Consultant makes any patentable inventions relating to the above project, Consultant agrees to be named as an applicant in any US patent application(s) filed on such invention(s). Actual ownership of such patent applications shall be governed by clause 8.

9B. Consultant shall promptly disclose to Contractor in writing all information pertaining to any intellectual property generated or conceived by Consultant under this Agreement. Consultant hereby assigns and agrees to assign all of Consultant's rights to such intellectual property, including patent rights and foreign priority rights. Consultant hereby expressly agrees, without further charge for time, to do all things and sign all documents deemed by Contractor to be necessary or appropriate to invest in intellectual property, including obtaining for and vesting in Contractor all U.S. and foreign patents and patent applications which Contractor desires to obtain to cover such intellectual property, provided that Contractor shall bear all expenses relating thereto. All reasonable local travel time and expenses shall be borne by Consultant.

10. **Trade Secrets:** Consultant recognizes that all information relating to the above Project disclosed to Consultant by Contractor, and all information generated by Consultant in the performance of the above Work, is a valuable trade secret of Contractor and Consultant shall treat all such information as strictly confidential, during and after the performance of Work under this Agreement. Specifically Consultant shall not reveal, publish, or communicate any such information to anyone other than Contractor, and shall safeguard all such information from access to anyone other than Contractor, except upon the express written authorization of Contractor. This clause shall not apply to any information which Consultant can document in writing is presently in or enters the public domain from a bona fide source other than Consultant.

11. **Return Of Property:** Consultant agree to return all written materials and objects received from Contractor, to deliver to Contractor all objects and a copy (and all copies and originals if requested by Contractor) of all written materials resulting from or relating to work performed under this Agreement, and not to deliver to any person, organization, or publisher, or cause to be published, any such written material without prior written authorization.

12. **Conflicts Of Interest:** Consultant recognizes a fiduciary obligation to Contractor arising out of the work and services performed under this agreement and accordingly will not offer Consultant's service to or perform services for any competitor, potential or actual, of Contractor for the above Project, or perform any other acts which may result in any conflict of interest by Consultant, during and after the term of this Agreement.

13. **Mediation And Arbitration:** If any dispute arises under this Agreement, the parties shall negotiate in good faith to settle such dispute. If the parties cannot resolve such dispute themselves, then either party may submit the dispute to mediation by a mediator approved by both parties. If the parties cannot agree to any mediator, or if either party does not wish to abide by any decision of the mediator, they shall submit the dispute to arbitration by any mutually-acceptable arbitrator, or the American Arbitration Association (AAA). If the AAA is selected, the arbitration shall take place under the auspices of the nearest branch of such to both parties. The costs of the arbitration proceeding shall be borne according to the decision of the arbitrator, who may apportion costs equally, or in accordance with any finding or fault or lack of good faith of either party. The arbitrator's award shall be non-appealable and enforceable in any court of competent jurisdiction.

14. **Governing Law:** This Agreement shall be governed by and interpreted under and according to the laws of the State of _____ .

15. **Signatures:** The parties have indicated their agreement to all of the above terms by signing this Agreement on the respective dates below indicated. Each party has received an original signed copy hereof.

Contractor:

Date: _____   _____

Consultant:

Date: _____   _____

Consultant's Work Agreement

1. **Parties:** This Work Agreement is made between the following parties:

   Name(s) _____

   Address(es): _____

   _____

   (hereinafter Contractor), and

   Name(s): _____

   Address(es): _____

   _____

   (hereinafter Consultant).

2. **Name of Project:** _____

   _____

   _____

3. **Work To Be Performed By Consultant:** _____

   _____

   _____

4. **Work/Payment Schedule:** _____

   _____

   _____

5. **Date:** This Agreement shall be effective as of the latter date below written.

6. **Recitals:** Contractor has one or more ideas relating to the above project and desires to have such project developed more completely, as specified in the above statement of Work. Consultant has certain skills desired by Contractor relating to performance of the above Work.

7. **Performance:** Consultant will perform the above work for Contractor, in accordance with the above-scheduled Work/Payment Schedule and Contractor will make the above scheduled payments to Consultant. Any changes to the Work To Be Performed or the Work/Payment Schedule shall be described in a writing referring to this Agreement and signed and dated by both parties. Time is of the essence of this Agreement, and if Consultant fails to perform according to the above work schedule, contractor may (a) void this agreement and pay consultant 50% of what would otherwise be due, or (b) require that Consultant pay contractor a penalty of $_____ per day.

8. **Intellectual Property:** All intellectual property, including trademarks, writings, information, trade secrets, inventions, discoveries, or improvements, whether or not registerable or patentable, which are conceived, constructed, or written by Consultant and arise out of or are related to work and services performed under this agreement, are, or shall become and remain the sole and exclusive property of Contractor, whether or not such intellectual property is conceived during the time such work and services are performed or billed.

9A. **Protection Of Intellectual Property:** Contractor and Consultant recognize that under US patent laws, all patent applications must be filed in the name of the true and actual inventor(s) of the subject matter sought to be patented. Thus if Consultant makes any patentable inventions relating to the above project, Consultant agrees to be named as an applicant in any US patent application(s) filed on such invention(s). Actual ownership of such patent applications shall be governed by clause 8.

9B. Consultant shall promptly disclose to Contractor in writing all information pertaining to any intellectual property generated or conceived by Consultant under this Agreement. Consultant hereby assigns and agrees to assign all of Consultant's rights to such intellectual property, including patent rights and foreign priority rights. Consultant hereby expressly agrees, without further charge for time, to do all things and sign all documents deemed by Contractor to be necessary or appropriate to invest in intellectual property, including obtaining for and vesting in Contractor all U.S. and foreign patents and patent applications which Contractor desires to obtain to cover such intellectual property, provided that Contractor shall bear all expenses relating thereto. All reasonable local travel time and expenses shall be borne by Consultant.

10. **Trade Secrets:** Consultant recognizes that all information relating to the above Project disclosed to Consultant by Contractor, and all information generated by Consultant in the performance of the above Work, is a valuable trade secret of Contractor and Consultant shall treat all such information as strictly confidential, during and after the performance of Work under this Agreement. Specifically Consultant shall not reveal, publish, or communicate any such information to anyone other than Contractor, and shall safeguard all such information from access to anyone other than Contractor, except upon the express written authorization of Contractor. This clause shall not apply to any information which Consultant can document in writing is presently in or enters the public domain from a bona fide source other than Consultant.

11. **Return Of Property:** Consultant agree to return all written materials and objects received from Contractor, to deliver to Contractor all objects and a copy (and all copies and originals if requested by Contractor) of all written materials resulting from or relating to work performed under this Agreement, and not to deliver to any person, organization, or publisher, or cause to be published, any such written material without prior written authorization.

12. **Conflicts Of Interest:** Consultant recognizes a fiduciary obligation to Contractor arising out of the work and services performed under this agreement and accordingly will not offer Consultant's service to or perform services for any competitor, potential or actual, of Contractor for the above Project, or perform any other acts which may result in any conflict of interest by Consultant, during and after the term of this Agreement.

13. **Mediation And Arbitration:** If any dispute arises under this Agreement, the parties shall negotiate in good faith to settle such dispute. If the parties cannot resolve such dispute themselves, then either party may submit the dispute to mediation by a mediator approved by both parties. If the parties cannot agree to any mediator, or if either party does not wish to abide by any decision of the mediator, they shall submit the dispute to arbitration by any mutually-acceptable arbitrator, or the American Arbitration Association (AAA). If the AAA is selected, the arbitration shall take place under the auspices of the nearest branch of such to both parties. The costs of the arbitration proceeding shall be borne according to the decision of the arbitrator, who may apportion costs equally, or in accordance with any finding or fault or lack of good faith of either party. The arbitrator's award shall be non-appealable and enforceable in any court of competent jurisdiction.

14. **Governing Law:** This Agreement shall be governed by and interpreted under and according to the laws of the State of _____ .

15. **Signatures:** The parties have indicated their agreement to all of the above terms by signing this Agreement on the respective dates below indicated. Each party has received an original signed copy hereof.

Contractor:

Date: _____   _____

Consultant:

Date: _____   _____

Proprietary Materials Agreement
(Keep Confidential/Non-Disclosure Agreement)

PROPRIETARY MATERIALS (items, documents, or models loaned—describe or identify fully): _____

_____

_____

_____

PROPRIETARY MATERIALS loaned by (name and address):_____

_____ ("LENDER")

PROPRIETARY MATERIALS loaned to (name and address): _____

_____ ("BORROWER")

BORROWER acknowledges and agrees as follows:

(1) Borrower:

    (a) has received the above Proprietary Materials from Lender (____)

    (b) understands that LENDER will immediately send the above PROPRIETARY MATERIALS to BORROWER upon LENDER'S receipt, from BORROWER, of a signed copy of this Agreement (___)

    [BORROWER cross out (a) and initial (b), or vice-versa, as appropriate]

(2) These PROPRIETARY MATERIALS contain valuable proprietary information of LENDER. This proprietary information constitutes a trade secret of LENDER and loss or outside disclosure of these materials or the information contained within these materials will harm lender economically.

(3) BORROWER acknowledges that these PROPRIETARY MATERIALS are furnished to BORROWER under the following conditions:

    (a) These PROPRIETARY MATERIALS and the information they contain shall be used by BORROWER solely to review or evaluate a proposal or information from, supply a quotation to, or provide a component or item for LENDER.

    (b) BORROWER agrees not to disclose these PROPRIETARY MATERIALS or the information they contain except to any persons with in BORROWER'S organization having a good faith "need to know" same for the purpose of fulfilling the terms of this Agreement. If necessary, BORROWER may make additional copies of this Agreement and have each such person sign a copy of this Agreement and furnish such copy(ies) to LENDER.

    (c) BORROWER and all persons within BORROWER'S organization shall exercise a high degree of care to safeguard these PROPRIETARY MATERIALS and the information they contain from access or disclosure to all unauthorized persons.

    (d) BORROWER shall not make any copies of these PROPRIETARY MATERIALS except upon written permission of LENDER and BORROWER shall return all PROPRIETARY MATERIALS (including any copies made) to LENDER at any time upon request by LENDER.

(4) These terms shall not apply to any information which BORROWER can document becomes part of these general public knowledge without fault of BORROWER or comes into BORROWER'S possession in good faith without restriction.

BORROWER: _____
(Name of Organization or Individual)

By: _____

_____
(Name and Title)

Date: ____/____/____

Other persons within BORROWER'S organization obtaining access to PROPRIETARY MATERIALS:

_____   ____/____/____

Print Name: _____

_____   ____/____/____

Print Name: _____

Proprietary Materials Agreement
(Keep Confidential/Non-Disclosure Agreement)

PROPRIETARY MATERIALS (items, documents, or models loaned—describe or identify fully): _____

_____

_____

_____

PROPRIETARY MATERIALS loaned by (name and address): _____

_____ ("LENDER")

PROPRIETARY MATERIALS loaned to (name and address): _____

_____ ("BORROWER")

BORROWER acknowledges and agrees as follows:

(1) Borrower:

    (a) has received the above Proprietary Materials from Lender (____)

    (b) understands that LENDER will immediately send the above PROPRIETARY MATERIALS to BORROWER upon LENDER'S receipt, from BORROWER, of a signed copy of this Agreement (____)

    [BORROWER cross out (a) and initial (b), or vice-versa, as appropriate]

(2) These PROPRIETARY MATERIALS contain valuable proprietary information of LENDER. This proprietary information constitutes a trade secret of LENDER and loss or outside disclosure of these materials or the information contained within these materials will harm lender economically.

(3) BORROWER acknowledges that these PROPRIETARY MATERIALS are furnished to BORROWER under the following conditions:

    (a) These PROPRIETARY MATERIALS and the information they contain shall be used by BORROWER solely to review or evaluate a proposal or information from, supply a quotation to, or provide a component or item for LENDER.

    (b) BORROWER agrees not to disclose these PROPRIETARY MATERIALS or the information they contain except to any persons with in BORROWER'S organization having a good faith "need to know" same for the purpose of fulfilling the terms of this Agreement. If necessary, BORROWER may make additional copies of this Agreement and have each such person sign a copy of this Agreement and furnish such copy(ies) to LENDER.

    (c) BORROWER and all persons within BORROWER'S organization shall exercise a high degree of care to safeguard these PROPRIETARY MATERIALS and the information they contain from access or disclosure to all unauthorized persons.

    (d) BORROWER shall not make any copies of these PROPRIETARY MATERIALS except upon written permission of LENDER and BORROWER shall return all PROPRIETARY MATERIALS (including any copies made) to LENDER at any time upon request by LENDER.

(4) These terms shall not apply to any information which BORROWER can document becomes part of these general public knowledge without fault of BORROWER or comes into BORROWER'S possession in good faith without restriction.

BORROWER: _____
                (Name of Organization or Individual)

By: _____

_____
                (Name and Title)

Date: ____/____/____

Other persons within BORROWER'S organization obtaining access to PROPRIETARY MATERIALS:

_____   ____/____/____

Print Name: _____

_____   ____/____/____

Print Name: _____

Proprietary Materials Agreement
(Keep Confidential/Non-Disclosure Agreement)

PROPRIETARY MATERIALS (items, documents, or models loaned-—describe or identify fully):_____

_____

_____

_____

PROPRIETARY MATERIALS loaned by (name and address):_____

_____ ("LENDER")

PROPRIETARY MATERIALS loaned to (name and address): _____

_____ ("BORROWER")

BORROWER acknowledges and agrees as follows:

(1) Borrower:

    (a) has received the above Proprietary Materials from Lender (____)

    (b) understands that LENDER will immediately send the above PROPRIETARY MATERIALS to BORROWER upon LENDER'S receipt, from BORROWER, of a signed copy of this Agreement (___)

    [BORROWER cross out (a) and initial (b), or vice-versa, as appropriate]

(2) These PROPRIETARY MATERIALS contain valuable proprietary information of LENDER. This proprietary information constitutes a trade secret of LENDER and loss or outside disclosure of these materials or the information contained within these materials will harm lender economically.

(3) BORROWER acknowledges that these PROPRIETARY MATERIALS are furnished to BORROWER under the following conditions:

    (a) These PROPRIETARY MATERIALS and the information they contain shall be used by BORROWER solely to review or evaluate a proposal or information from, supply a quotation to, or provide a component or item for LENDER.

    (b) BORROWER agrees not to disclose these PROPRIETARY MATERIALS or the information they contain except to any persons with in BORROWER'S organization having a good faith "need to know" same for the purpose of fulfilling the terms of this Agreement. If necessary, BORROWER may make additional copies of this Agreement and have each such person sign a copy of this Agreement and furnish such copy(ies) to LENDER.

    (c) BORROWER and all persons within BORROWER'S organization shall exercise a high degree of care to safeguard these PROPRIETARY MATERIALS and the information they contain from access or disclosure to all unauthorized persons.

    (d) BORROWER shall not make any copies of these PROPRIETARY MATERIALS except upon written permission of LENDER and BORROWER shall return all PROPRIETARY MATERIALS (including any copies made) to LENDER at any time upon request by LENDER.

(4) These terms shall not apply to any information which BORROWER can document becomes part of these general public knowledge without fault of BORROWER or comes into BORROWER'S possession in good faith without restriction.

BORROWER: _____
                    (Name of Organization or Individual)

By: _____

_____
                    (Name and Title)

Date: ____/____/____

Other persons within BORROWER'S organization obtaining access to PROPRIETARY MATERIALS:

_____   ____/____/____

Print Name: _____

_____   ____/____/____

Print Name: _____

Proprietary Materials Agreement
(Keep Confidential/Non-Disclosure Agreement)

PROPRIETARY MATERIALS (items, documents, or models loaned—describe or identify fully): _____

_____

_____

_____

PROPRIETARY MATERIALS loaned by (name and address):_____

_____ ("LENDER")

PROPRIETARY MATERIALS loaned to (name and address): _____

_____ ("BORROWER")

BORROWER acknowledges and agrees as follows:

(1) Borrower:

    (a) has received the above Proprietary Materials from Lender (____)

    (b) understands that LENDER will immediately send the above PROPRIETARY MATERIALS to BORROWER upon LENDER'S receipt, from BORROWER, of a signed copy of this Agreement (___)

    [BORROWER cross out (a) and initial (b), or vice-versa, as appropriate]

(2) These PROPRIETARY MATERIALS contain valuable proprietary information of LENDER. This proprietary information constitutes a trade secret of LENDER and loss or outside disclosure of these materials or the information contained within these materials will harm lender economically.

(3) BORROWER acknowledges that these PROPRIETARY MATERIALS are furnished to BORROWER under the following conditions:

    (a) These PROPRIETARY MATERIALS and the information they contain shall be used by BORROWER solely to review or evaluate a proposal or information from, supply a quotation to, or provide a component or item for LENDER.

    (b) BORROWER agrees not to disclose these PROPRIETARY MATERIALS or the information they contain except to any persons with in BORROWER'S organization having a good faith "need to know" same for the purpose of fulfilling the terms of this Agreement. If necessary, BORROWER may make additional copies of this Agreement and have each such person sign a copy of this Agreement and furnish such copy(ies) to LENDER.

    (c) BORROWER and all persons within BORROWER'S organization shall exercise a high degree of care to safeguard these PROPRIETARY MATERIALS and the information they contain from access or disclosure to all unauthorized persons.

    (d) BORROWER shall not make any copies of these PROPRIETARY MATERIALS except upon written permission of LENDER and BORROWER shall return all PROPRIETARY MATERIALS (including any copies made) to LENDER at any time upon request by LENDER.

(4) These terms shall not apply to any information which BORROWER can document becomes part of these general public knowledge without fault of BORROWER or comes into BORROWER'S possession in good faith without restriction.

BORROWER: _____

                (Name of Organization or Individual)

By: _____

_____

                (Name and Title)

Date: ____/____/____

Other persons within BORROWER'S organization obtaining access to PROPRIETARY MATERIALS:

_____   ____/____/____

Print Name: _____

_____   ____/____/____

Print Name: _____

Proprietary Materials Agreement
(Keep Confidential/Non-Disclosure Agreement)

PROPRIETARY MATERIALS (items, documents, or models loaned—describe or identify fully): _____

_____

_____

_____

PROPRIETARY MATERIALS loaned by (name and address):_____

_____ ("LENDER")

PROPRIETARY MATERIALS loaned to (name and address): _____

_____ ("BORROWER")

BORROWER acknowledges and agrees as follows:

(1) Borrower:

    (a) has received the above Proprietary Materials from Lender (_____)

    (b) understands that LENDER will immediately send the above PROPRIETARY MATERIALS to BORROWER upon LENDER'S receipt, from BORROWER, of a signed copy of this Agreement (___)

    [BORROWER cross out (a) and initial (b), or vice-versa, as appropriate]

(2) These PROPRIETARY MATERIALS contain valuable proprietary information of LENDER. This proprietary information constitutes a trade secret of LENDER and loss or outside disclosure of these materials or the information contained within these materials will harm lender economically.

(3) BORROWER acknowledges that these PROPRIETARY MATERIALS are furnished to BORROWER under the following conditions:

    (a) These PROPRIETARY MATERIALS and the information they contain shall be used by BORROWER solely to review or evaluate a proposal or information from, supply a quotation to, or provide a component or item for LENDER.

    (b) BORROWER agrees not to disclose these PROPRIETARY MATERIALS or the information they contain except to any persons with in BORROWER'S organization having a good faith "need to know" same for the purpose of fulfilling the terms of this Agreement. If necessary, BORROWER may make additional copies of this Agreement and have each such person sign a copy of this Agreement and furnish such copy(ies) to LENDER.

    (c) BORROWER and all persons within BORROWER'S organization shall exercise a high degree of care to safeguard these PROPRIETARY MATERIALS and the information they contain from access or disclosure to all unauthorized persons.

    (d) BORROWER shall not make any copies of these PROPRIETARY MATERIALS except upon written permission of LENDER and BORROWER shall return all PROPRIETARY MATERIALS (including any copies made) to LENDER at any time upon request by LENDER.

(4) These terms shall not apply to any information which BORROWER can document becomes part of these general public knowledge without fault of BORROWER or comes into BORROWER'S possession in good faith without restriction.

BORROWER: _____
(Name of Organization or Individual)

By: _____

_____
(Name and Title)

Date: ____/____/____

Other persons within BORROWER'S organization obtaining access to PROPRIETARY MATERIALS:

_____   ____/____/____

Print Name: _____

_____   ____/____/____

Print Name: _____

Positive and Negative Factors Evaluation

Inventor(s): _____

Invention: _____

_____

_____

Factor	Weight if Positive	Weight if Negative
1. Cost		
2. Weight		
3. Size		
4. Safety/Health		
5. Speed		
6. Ease of Use		
7. Ease of Production		
8. Durability		
9. Repairability		
10. Novelty		
11. Convenience/Social Benefit/Mechanization		
12. Reliability		
13. Ecology		
14. Salability		
15. Appearance		
16. Viewability		
17. Precision		
18. Noise		
19. Odor		
20. Taste		
21. Market Size		
22. Trend of Demand		
23. Seasonal Demand		
24. Difficulty of Market Penetration		
25. Potential Competition		
26. Quality		
27. Excitement		
28. Markup		

Factor	Weight if Positive	Weight if Negative
29. Inferior Performance		
30. "Sexy" Packaging		
31. Miscellaneous		
32. Long Life Cycle		
33. Related Product Addability		
34. Satisfies Existing Need		
35. Legality		
36. Operability		
37. Development		
38. Profitability		
39. Obsolescence		
40. Incompatability		
41. Product Liability Risk		
42. Market Dependence		
43. Difficulty of Distribution		
44. Service Requirements		
45. New Tooling Required		
46. Inertia Must Be Overcome		
47. Too Advanced Technically		
48. Substantial Learning Required		
49. Difficult To Promote		
50. Lack of Market		
51. Crowded Field		
52. Commodities		
53. Combination Products		
54. Entrenched Competition		
55. Instant Anachronism		

Total Positive _____

Less: Total Negative _____

NET: _____

Signed_____   Date: _____

Positive and Negative Factors Evaluation

Inventor(s): _____   Invention: _____

_____   _____

Factor	Weight if Positive	Weight if Negative
1. Cost		
2. Weight		
3. Size		
4. Safety/Health		
5. Speed		
6. Ease of Use		
7. Ease of Production		
8. Durability		
9. Repairability		
10. Novelty		
11. Convenience/Social Benefit/Mechanization		
12. Reliability		
13. Ecology		
14. Salability		
15. Appearance		
16. Viewability		
17. Precision		
18. Noise		
19. Odor		
20. Taste		
21. Market Size		
22. Trend of Demand		
23. Seasonal Demand		
24. Difficulty of Market Penetration		
25. Potential Competition		
26. Quality		
27. Excitement		
28. Markup		

Factor	Weight if Positive	Weight if Negative
29. Inferior Performance		
30. "Sexy" Packaging		
31. Miscellaneous		
32. Long Life Cycle		
33. Related Product Addability		
34. Satisfies Existing Need		
35. Legality		
36. Operability		
37. Development		
38. Profitability		
39. Obsolescence		
40. Incompatability		
41. Product Liability Risk		
42. Market Dependence		
43. Difficulty of Distribution		
44. Service Requirements		
45. New Tooling Required		
46. Inertia Must Be Overcome		
47. Too Advanced Technically		
48. Substantial Learning Required		
49. Difficult To Promote		
50. Lack of Market		
51. Crowded Field		
52. Commodities		
53. Combination Products		
54. Entrenched Competition		
55. Instant Anachronism		

Total Positive   _____

Less: Total Negative _____

NET: _____

Signed _____   Date: _____

Positive and Negative Factors Evaluation

Inventor(s): _____   Invention: _____

_____   _____

Factor	Weight if Positive	Weight if Negative
1. Cost		
2. Weight		
3. Size		
4. Safety/Health		
5. Speed		
6. Ease of Use		
7. Ease of Production		
8. Durability		
9. Repairability		
10. Novelty		
11. Convenience/Social Benefit/Mechanization		
12. Reliability		
13. Ecology		
14. Salability		
15. Appearance		
16. Viewability		
17. Precision		
18. Noise		
19. Odor		
20. Taste		
21. Market Size		
22. Trend of Demand		
23. Seasonal Demand		
24. Difficulty of Market Penetration		
25. Potential Competition		
26. Quality		
27. Excitement		
28. Markup		

Factor	Weight if Positive	Weight if Negative
29. Inferior Performance		
30. "Sexy" Packaging		
31. Miscellaneous		
32. Long Life Cycle		
33. Related Product Addability		
34. Satisfies Existing Need		
35. Legality		
36. Operability		
37. Development		
38. Profitability		
39. Obsolescence		
40. Incompatability		
41. Product Liability Risk		
42. Market Dependence		
43. Difficulty of Distribution		
44. Service Requirements		
45. New Tooling Required		
46. Inertia Must Be Overcome		
47. Too Advanced Technically		
48. Substantial Learning Required		
49. Difficult To Promote		
50. Lack of Market		
51. Crowded Field		
52. Commodities		
53. Combination Products		
54. Entrenched Competition		
55. Instant Anachronism		

Total Positive   _____

Less: Total Negative   _____

NET: _____

Signed _____   Date: _____

Positive and Negative Factors Evaluation

Inventor(s): _____   Invention: _____

_____   _____

Factor	Weight if Positive	Weight if Negative
1. Cost		
2. Weight		
3. Size		
4. Safety/Health		
5. Speed		
6. Ease of Use		
7. Ease of Production		
8. Durability		
9. Repairability		
10. Novelty		
11. Convenience/Social Benefit/Mechanization		
12. Reliability		
13. Ecology		
14. Salability		
15. Appearance		
16. Viewability		
17. Precision		
18. Noise		
19. Odor		
20. Taste		
21. Market Size		
22. Trend of Demand		
23. Seasonal Demand		
24. Difficulty of Market Penetration		
25. Potential Competition		
26. Quality		
27. Excitement		
28. Markup		

Factor	Weight if Positive	Weight if Negative
29. Inferior Performance		
30. "Sexy" Packaging		
31. Miscellaneous		
32. Long Life Cycle		
33. Related Product Addability		
34. Satisfies Existing Need		
35. Legality		
36. Operability		
37. Development		
38. Profitability		
39. Obsolescence		
40. Incompatability		
41. Product Liability Risk		
42. Market Dependence		
43. Difficulty of Distribution		
44. Service Requirements		
45. New Tooling Required		
46. Inertia Must Be Overcome		
47. Too Advanced Technically		
48. Substantial Learning Required		
49. Difficult To Promote		
50. Lack of Market		
51. Crowded Field		
52. Commodities		
53. Combination Products		
54. Entrenched Competition		
55. Instant Anachronism		

Total Positive   _____

Less: Total Negative   _____

NET: _____

Signed _____   Date: _____

CATALOG

...more from Nolo Press

Book with disk

TO ORDER CALL 800-992-6656

	EDITION	PRICE	CODE
The Partnership Book: How to Write a Partnership Agreement.................... 4th		$24.95	PART
Trademark: How to Name Your Business & Product............................. 1st		$29.95	TRD

CONSUMER

	EDITION	PRICE	CODE
Fed Up With the Legal System: What's Wrong & How to Fix It 2nd		$9.95	LEG
Glossary of Insurance Terms 5th		$14.95	GLINT
How to Win Your Personal Injury Claim 1st		$24.95	PICL
Nolo's Law Form Kit: Hiring Child Care & Household Help 1st		$14.95	KCHLD
Nolo's Pocket Guide to California Law 3rd		$10.95	CLAW
Nolo's Pocket Guide to California Law on Disk—Windows 3.0		$17.46	CLW3
Nolo's Pocket Guide to Consumer Rights (California Edition)..................... 2nd		$12.95	CAG
The Over 50 Insurance Survival Guide 1st		$16.95	OVER50
What Do You Mean It's Not Covered?... 1st		$19.95	COVER

ESTATE PLANNING & PROBATE

	EDITION	PRICE	CODE
5 Ways to Avoid Probate—Audio... 1st		$14.95	TPRO
How to Probate an Estate (California Edition) 8th		$34.95	PAE
Make Your Own Living Trust... 1st		$19.95	LITR
Nolo's Law Form Kit: Wills 1st		$14.95	KWL
Nolo's Simple Will Book.. 2nd		$17.95	SWIL
Plan Your Estate 3rd		$24.95	NEST
Write Your Will—Audio.. 1st		$14.95	TWYW

FAMILY MATTERS

	EDITION	PRICE	CODE
A Legal Guide for Lesbian and Gay Couples...................................... 8th		$24.95	LG
Child Custody: Building Agreements that Work 1st		$24.95	CUST
Divorce & Money: How to Make the Best Financial Decisions During Divorce 2nd		$21.95	DIMO
How to Adopt Your Stepchild in California 4th		$22.95	ADOP
How to Do Your Own Divorce in California 20th		$21.95	CDIV
How to Do Your Own Divorce in Texas 5th		$17.95	TDIV
How to Raise or Lower Child Support in California 3rd		$18.95	CHLD
Nolo's Pocket Guide to Family Law 3rd		$14.95	FLD

 Book with disk

TO ORDER CALL 800-992-6656

	EDITION	PRICE	CODE
Practical Divorce Solutions 1st		$14.95	PDS
The Guardianship Book (California Edition) 2nd		$24.95	GB
The Living Together Kit.. 7th		$24.95	LTK

GOING TO COURT

	EDITION	PRICE	CODE
Collect Your Court Judgment (California Edition)................................. 2nd		$19.95	JUDG
Everybody's Guide to Municipal Court (California Edition) 1st		$29.95	MUNI
Everybody's Guide to Small Claims Court (California Edition)...................... 11th		$18.95	CSCC
Everybody's Guide to Small Claims Court (National Edition) 5th		$18.95	NSCC
Fight Your Ticket ... and Win! (California Edition)................................. 6th		$19.95	FYT
How to Change Your Name (California Edition)................................. 6th		$24.95	NAME
Represent Yourself in Court: How to Prepare & Try a Winning Case 1st		$29.95	RYC
The Criminal Records Book (California Edition)................................. 4th		$21.95	CRIM
Winning in Small Claims Court—Audio 1st		$14.95	TWIN

HOMEOWNERS, LANDLORDS & TENANTS

	EDITION	PRICE	CODE
Dog Law 2nd		$12.95	DOG
For Sale by Owner (California Edition).. 2nd		$24.95	FSBO
Homestead Your House (California Edition) 8th		$9.95	HOME
How to Buy a House in California.. 3rd		$24.95	BHCA
Neighbor Law: Fences, Trees, Boundaries & Noise............................... 2nd		$16.95	NEI
Nolo's Law Form Kit: Leases & Rental Agreements (California Edition) 1st		$14.95	KLEAS
Safe Homes, Safe Neighborhoods: Stopping Crime Where You Live............... 1st		$14.95	SAFE
Tenants' Rights (California Edition) 12th		$18.95	CTEN
The Deeds Book (California Edition).. 3rd		$16.95	DEED
The Landlord's Law Book, Vol. 1: Rights & Responsibilities (California Edition)....... 4th		$32.95	LBRT
The Landlord's Law Book, Vol. 2: Evictions (California Edition).................... 5th		$34.95	LBEV

HUMOR

	EDITION	PRICE	CODE
29 Reasons Not to Go to Law School.. 4th		$9.95	29R
Devil's Advocates: The Unnatural History of Lawyers............................. 1st		$12.95	DA
Nolo's Favorite Lawyer Jokes On Disk—DOS 1.0		$9.95	JODI

 Book with disk

TO ORDER CALL 800-992-6656

	EDITION	PRICE	CODE
Nolo's Favorite Lawyer Jokes On Disk—Macintosh	1.0	$9.95	JODM
Nolo's Favorite Lawyer Jokes On Disk—Windows	1st	$9.95	JODWI
Poetic Justice: The Funniest, Meanest Things Ever Said About Lawyers	1st	$9.95	PJ

IMMIGRATION

	EDITION	PRICE	CODE
Como Obtener La Tarjeta Verde: Maneras Legitimas de Permanecer en los EE.UU.	1st	$24.95	VERDE
How to Become a United States Citizen	5th	$14.95	CIT
How to Get a Green Card: Legal Ways to Stay in the U.S.A.	1st	$22.95	GRN

MONEY MATTERS

	EDITION	PRICE	CODE
Chapter 13 Bankruptcy: Repay Your Debts	1st	$29.95	CH13
How to File for Bankruptcy	5th	$25.95	HFB
Money Troubles: Legal Strategies to Cope With Your Debts	3rd	$18.95	MT
Nolo's Law Form Kit: Buy & Sell Contracts	1st	$9.95	KCONT
Nolo's Law Form Kit: Loan Agreements	1st	$14.95	KLOAN
Nolo's Law Form Kit: Personal Bankruptcy	1st	$14.95	KBNK
Nolo's Law Form Kit: Power of Attorney	1st	$14.95	KPA
Nolo's Law Form Kit: Rebuild Your Credit	1st	$14.95	KCRD
Simple Contracts for Personal Use	2nd	$16.95	CONT
Smart Ways to Save Money During and After Divorce	1st	$14.95	SAVMO
Stand Up to the IRS	2nd	$21.95	SIRS

PATENTS AND COPYRIGHTS

	EDITION	PRICE	CODE
Copyright Your Software	1st	$39.95	CYS
Patent It Yourself	3rd	$39.95	PAT
💾 Software Development: A Legal Guide (Book with disk—PC)	1st	$44.95	SFT
The Copyright Handbook: How to Protect and Use Written Works	2nd	$24.95	COHA
The Inventor's Notebook	1st	$19.95	INOT

RESEARCH & REFERENCE

	EDITION	PRICE	CODE
Law on the Net	1st	$39.95	LAWN
Legal Research: How to Find & Understand the Law	4th	$19.95	LRES
Legal Research Made Easy: A Roadmap through the Law Library Maze—Video	1st	$89.95	LRME

💾 Book with disk

TO ORDER CALL 800-992-6656

	EDITION	PRICE	CODE

SENIORS

	EDITION	PRICE	CODE
Beat the Nursing Home Trap: A Consumer's Guide	2nd	$18.95	ELD
Social Security, Medicare & Pensions: The Sourcebook for Older Americans	5th	$18.95	SOA
The Conservatorship Book (California Edition)	2nd	$29.95	CNSV

SOFTWARE

	EDITION	PRICE	CODE
California Incorporator 1.0—DOS	1.0	$90.30	INCI
Living Trust Maker 2.0—Macintosh	2.0	$55.96	LTM2
Living Trust Maker 2.0—Windows	2.0	$55.96	LTWI2
Nolo's Partnership Maker 1.0—DOS	1.0	$90.96	PAGII
Nolo's Personal RecordKeeper 3.0—Macintosh	3.0	$34.96	FRM3
Patent It Yourself 1.0—Windows	1.0	$160.96	PYWI
WillMaker 5.0—DOS	5.0	$48.96	WI5
WillMaker 5.0—Macintosh	5.0	$48.96	WM5
WillMaker 5.0—Windows	5.0	$48.96	WIW5

WORKPLACE

	EDITION	PRICE	CODE
How to Handle Your Workers' Compensation Claim (California Edition)	1st	$29.95	WORK
Rightful Termination	1st	$29.95	RITE
Sexual Harassment on the Job	2nd	$18.95	HARS
Workers' Comp for Employers	2nd	$29.95	CNTRL
Your Rights in the Workplace	2nd	$15.95	YRW

TO ORDER CALL 800-992-6656

ORDER FORM

Code	Quantity	Title	Unit price	Total

Subtotal	
California residents add Sales Tax	
Shipping & Handling ($4 for 1st item; $1 each additional)	
2nd day UPS (additional $5; $8 in Alaska and Hawaii)	
TOTAL	

Name

Address

(UPS to street address, Priority Mail to P.O. boxes)

FOR FASTER SERVICE, USE YOUR CREDIT CARD AND OUR TOLL-FREE NUMBERS

Monday-Friday, 7 a.m. to 6 p.m. Pacific Time

Order Line   1 (800) 992-6656 (in the 510 area code, call 549-1976)

General Information 1 (510) 549-1976

Fax your order   1 (800) 645-0895 (in the 510 area code, call 548-5902)

METHOD OF PAYMENT

☐ Check enclosed

☐ VISA   ☐ MasterCard   ☐ Discover Card   ☐ American Express

Account #   Expiration Date

Authorizing Signature

Daytime Phone

Allow 2-3 weeks for delivery. Prices subject to change.

INOT 1.5

NOLO PRESS, 950 PARKER ST., BERKELEY, CA 94710

New!

Patent It Yourself Software

A stand-alone program that helps you prepare, file and prosecute your own patent application.

Includes:

- a fully searchable on-line version of the best-seller *Patent It Yourself* by Attorney David Pressman
- real patents as models for good patent drafting
- different tracks for expert and novice users
- all forms needed to document and file a patent
- contracts for hiring outside help on your patent project

System requirements: Any PC running Microsoft Windows 3.1

For more information: call 1-800-992-6656
or write Nolo Press, 950 Parker Street, Berkeley, CA 94710

NOLO PRESS

GET 25% OFF
YOUR NEXT PURCHASE

RECYCLE YOUR OUT-OF-DATE BOOKS

It's important to have the most current legal information. Because laws and legal procedures change often, we update our books regularly. To help keep you up-to-date we are extending this special offer. Cut out and mail the title portion of the cover of any old Nolo book with your next order and we'll give you a 25% discount off the retail price of ANY new Nolo book you purchase directly from us. For current prices and editions call us at 1-800-992-6656.

This offer is to individuals only.

Take 2 minutes & Get a 2-year NOLO *News* subscription free!*

CALL
1-800-992-6656

FAX
1-800-645-0895

E-MAIL
NOLOSUB@NOLOPRESS.com

OR MAIL US THIS POSTAGE-PAID REGISTRATION CARD

NOLO *News*
SPRING 1994
Legal & Consumer Information for Everyone

Work-place Rights

INSIDE
10 THINGS BILL COLLECTORS DON'T WANT YOU TO KNOW
KEEPING LEGAL FEES DOWN DURING DIVORCE
WHERE TO FIND NOLO ONLINE
NEW BOOKS FROM NOLO
SMART WAYS TO SAVE MONEY DURING AND AFTER DIVORCE
TAKING CARE OF YOUR CORPORATION VOLUME 1: DIRECTOR & SHAREHOLDER MEETINGS MADE EASY (WITH FORMS ON DISK)

CATALOG INSIDE!

NOLO PRESS

With our quarterly magazine, the **NOLO** *News*, you'll
- **Learn** about important legal changes that affect you
- **Find out first** about new Nolo products
- **Keep current** with practical articles on everyday law
- **Get answers** to your legal questions in *Ask Auntie Nolo's* advice column
- **Save money** with special Subscriber Only discounts
- **Tickle your funny bone** with our famous *Lawyer Joke* column.

It only takes 2 minutes to reserve your free 2-year subscription or to extend your **NOLO** *News* subscription.

REGISTRATION CARD

NAME _____ DATE _____

ADDRESS _____

_____ PHONE NUMBER _____

CITY _____ STATE _____ ZIP _____

WHERE DID YOU HEAR ABOUT THIS BOOK? _____

WHERE DID YOU PURCHASE THIS PRODUCT? _____

DID YOU CONSULT A LAWYER? (PLEASE CIRCLE ONE)   YES   NO   NOT APPLICABLE

DID YOU FIND THIS BOOK HELPFUL?   (VERY)   5   4   3   2   1   (NOT AT ALL)

SUGGESTIONS FOR IMPROVING THIS PRODUCT _____

WAS IT EASY TO USE?   (VERY EASY)   5   4   3   2   1   (VERY DIFFICULT)

DO YOU OWN A COMPUTER? IF SO, WHICH FORMAT? (PLEASE CIRCLE ONE)   WINDOWS   DOS   MAC

INOT 1.5

"Nolo helps lay people perform legal tasks without the aid—or fees—of lawyers."

—USA TODAY

[Nolo books are ..."written in plain language, free of legal mumbo jumbo, and spiced with witty personal observations."

—ASSOCIATED PRESS

"...Nolo publications...guide people simply through the how, when, where and why of law."

—WASHINGTON POST

"Increasingly, people who are not lawyers are performing tasks usually regarded as legal work... And consumers, using books like Nolo's, do routine legal work themselves."

—NEW YORK TIMES

"...All of [Nolo's] books are easy-to-understand, are updated regularly, provide pull-out forms...and are often quite moving in their sense of compassion for the struggles of the lay reader."

—SAN FRANCISCO CHRONICLE